Forgotten
Founding
Father

OTHER BOOKS IN THE LEADERS IN ACTION SERIES

Forgotten Founding Father

THE HEROIC LEGACY OF
GEORGE WHITEFIELD

STEPHEN MANSFIELD

LEADERS IN ACTION
GENERAL EDITOR, GEORGE GRANT

CUMBERLAND HOUSE
NASHVILLE, TENNESSEE

Published by Cumberland House Publishing, Inc., 431 Harding Industrial Drive, Nashville, Tennessee 37211.

Library of Congress Cataloging-in-Publication Data

Mansfield, Stephen, 1958–
  Forgotten founding father : the heroic legacy of George
    Whitefield / Douglas Wilson.
      p. cm. — (Leaders in action)
  Includes bibliographical references.
  ISBN-13 978-1-58182-165-9; ISBN-10 1-58182-165-4 (alk. paper)
    1. Whitefield, George, 1714–1770. 2. Evangelists—England—
  Biography. 3. Evangelists—United States—Biography. I. Title.
  II. Leaders in action series.
  BX9225.W4 M36 2001
  269'.2'092—dc21
  [B]   2001028211

Printed in the United States of America

2 3 4 5 6 7 8 9—10 09 08 07

*To the young lions
who will soon lead us
into the Greatest Awakening*

CONTENTS

FOREWORD

*H*E WAS America's first celebrity. Though just twenty-five years old when he began touring the sparsely settled colonies in 1738, George Whitefield was an immediate sensation. And he remained so for the rest of his life. Over the next thirty years, amidst some seven visits from his native England, he would leave his mark on the lives of virtually every English-speaking soul living on this side of the Atlantic—from the cosmopolitan businessmen of Philadelphia and the seasoned traders of Boston to the yeoman farmers of Virginia and the frontier adventurers of Canada.

He literally took America by storm. "When he arrived in the colonies," says historian Mark Noll, "he was simply an event."[1] Wherever he went, vast crowds gathered to hear him. Commerce would cease. Shops would close. Farmers would leave their plows midfurrow. And affairs of the greatest import would be postponed. One of his sermons in the Boston Common actually drew more listeners than the city's entire population. Another in Philadelphia spilled over onto more than a dozen city blocks. Still another in Savannah recorded the largest single crowd ever to gather anywhere in the colonies—despite the scant local population.

Some said he blazed across the public firmament like a "heavenly comet."[2] Some said he was "a magnificent fascination of the like heretofore unknown."[3] Others said he "startled the world awake like a bolt from the blue."[4] There can be little doubt that he lived up to his reputation as "the marvel of the age."[5] As historian Harry Stout has written: "He was a preacher capable of commanding mass audiences—and offerings—across two continents, without any institutional support, through the sheer power of his personality. Whitefield wrote best-selling journals and drew audiences totaling in the millions. White and black, male and female, friends and enemies—all flocked in unprecedented numbers to hear the Grand Itinerant. Whenever he visited, people could do anything, it seemed, but stay away."[6]

All the greatest men of the day were in unabashed awe of his oratorical prowess. Shakespearean actor David Garrick said, "I would give a hundred guineas if I could say *oh* like Mr. Whitefield."[7] Benjamin Franklin once quipped, "He can bring men to tears merely by pronouncing the word *Mesopotamia*."[8] And Sarah Edwards—the astute and unaffected wife of the dean of American theologians, Jonathan Edwards—remarked, "He is a born orator."[9]

Yet despite his wide acclaim and popularity, Whitefield was often ridiculed, scorned, and persecuted for his faith. Hecklers blew trumpets and shouted obscenities at him as he preached. Enraged mobs often attacked his meetings, robbing, beating, and humiliating his followers. Men were maimed. Women were stripped and occasionally raped. Whitefield himself was subjected to unimaginable brutality—he was clubbed twice, stoned once, whipped at least half a dozen times, and beaten a half dozen more. And he lived constantly under the pall of death threats. Once, he recorded in his journal: "I was honored with having a few stones, dirt, rotten eggs, and pieces of dead cats thrown at me. Nevertheless, the Lord was gracious, and a great number were awakened unto life."[10]

Amazingly, it was not just the profane who condemned Whitefield's work. He was also opposed by the religious establishment. Accused of being "a fanatic," of being "intolerant," and of "flaming the flames" of "vile bigotry," he was often in "more danger of attack from the clergy than he was from the worldly."[11]

As a result, biographer Arnold Dallimore says, "Whitefield's entire evangelistic life was an evidence of his physical courage."[12] He fearlessly faced his opposition and continued his work. Though often stung by the vehemence of the opposition he faced, he refused to take it personally, attributing it rather to "the offense of the Gospel."[13]

He was, in short, the embodiment of the American pioneer: vibrant, passionate, stalwart, accomplished, principled, courageous, and wise. Indeed, his daily disposition became the model for the American character. By all accounts, he was "the father of modern evangelism."[14] He sparked a revival of portentous proportions—the Great Awakening.[15] He pioneered one of the most enduring church reform movements—Methodism.[16] And he laid the foundations for perhaps the greatest experiment in liberty the world has yet known—the American Republic.[17]

George Washington said, "Upon his lips the Gospel appears even to the coarsest of men as sweet and as true as, in fact, it is."[18] Patrick Henry mused, "Would that every bearer of God's glad tidings be as fit a vessel of grace as Mr. Whitefield."[19] And the poet, John Greenleaf Whittier, wrote of him:

> *That life of pure intent,*
> *That voice of warning, yet eloquent,*
> *Of one on the errands of angels sent.*[20]

He became, as Stephen Mansfield asserts in this sketch of his leadership qualities, the father of America's founding fathers. That he is largely forgotten today is therefore all the more tragic. That Dr. Mansfield has recovered his legacy is therefore all the more significant.

By offering us a fresh and vivid perspective of Whitefield's accomplishments, personal life, character, and struggles, Dr. Mansfield has produced a book that is not merely a compelling biography of a bygone hero, he has exposed for us the foundations of our heritage. As in his previous works on Winston Churchill and Booker T. Washington, he has demonstrated not only that he is a masterful storyteller, a careful historian, and an insightful analyst, he also shows us that he understands how the unfolding of past providence is not merely a review of antedated events but a preview of what should be, what could be, if only we would heed the lessons of our own legacy.

It is thus an apt and welcome addition to his already rich contributions to the Leaders in Action series. Indeed, it is an apt and welcome addition to the essential annals of Christian moral philosophy.

—George Grant

Acknowledgments

THE GRATITUDE of a lifetime I offer to Wayne Palmer for teaching me spiritual passion, to Kevin Ikenberry for teaching me the beauty of knowledge, to Oral Roberts for teaching me conviction, to David Toberty for teaching me how to laugh, to Bob Stamps for teaching me tradition, to Greg Webb for teaching me to live large, to Peter Marshall for teaching me providence, to Wilma Carter for teaching me Jesus, to Ryan Rowlands for trying—desperately—to teach me racquetball, to Rousas Rushdoony for teaching me history, to Walter Judd for teaching me greatness, to Don Finto for teaching me simplicity, to George Grant for simply teaching me, and to those who are my critics for being the unpaid guardians of my soul.

INTRODUCTION

*I*T HAD never been done. Perhaps it never would be. Perhaps it was impossible. After all, for generations men had dreamed of it, trained for it, and made it their measure of manhood. But no one had done it. No one had ever run the mile in less than four minutes.

Then it happened. On May 6, 1954, an Oxford medical student by the name of Roger Bannister made history by breaking the four-minute mile. The news was electrifying. A man had finally broken the legendary barrier. Men could hardly grasp the meaning of it.

Before long, people began to wonder if it would ever happen again. Maybe the four-minute mile was the final barrier. After all, it could be decades before someone else even matched Bannister's historic record, much less exceeded it.

But it only took six weeks. Indeed, a mere month and a half after Bannister's triumph, another man ran the mile in less than four minutes. What is more, within a few years, nearly half a dozen men had broken the once unbreakable barrier.

How could it be? How could so many people break such a long-standing record in such a short period of time?

Clearly, something about Roger Bannister's deed made it possible for men to run faster than they had ever run before. Somehow Bannister had broken a barrier of the mind or the spirit, had pierced the dark borders of impossibility and made a way for others to invade the realms of promise. Now, all who dared were free to press beyond the limits of the past and to redefine the best man could be. Many did, and it changed our world. Today, it is not uncommon for a college student to break the four-minute mile during a routine after-school practice. But it first took a Roger Bannister to make commonplace the once unattainable.

I love this story and I love it because of what it illustrates about heroes. Today, we use the word hero to describe anyone who is merely famous. In modern thinking, just to be well known makes a man a *hero* no matter what devastation he leaves in his wake. Think of today's rock stars: talented, globally famous, and often astonishingly destructive. People like these are heroes in the ancient Greek sense: they possess great gift and power yet are ruled by passion and bound by folly.

Instead, I love the Hebraic view of the hero. The ancient Hebrews used the word *hero* to describe men and women who by extraordinary character and conviction not only live lives of exceptional impact but also lift barriers of mind and spirit for generations after. Though flawed and beleaguered, these heroes shape their age through traits that others can emulate, thus leaving in their wake both a better world and lessons of the kind of character that make that better world possible.

It is just this view of the heroic that I had in mind when I decided to write about George Whitefield.* At a

---

* Whitefield is pronounced "Witfield." The "i" is short.

time when reasonable men doubted whether Christianity would survive in the English-speaking world, Whitefield both lived and proclaimed the gospel of Christ in such a manner as to lift the canopy of darkness in his generation. Through him, nations were transformed, revolutions were kindled, institutions were refashioned, and millions of lives were reclaimed for a higher call. What is more, a vibrant Christian faith continued to shape the English-speaking world for generations after. In other words, he changed his world and showed us how to do the same. This is what heroes do.

In an age that scoffs at true heroism, I am not ashamed to say that George Whitefield is one of my heroes. I admire him deeply. I am thankful for the legacy he left us. But I don't just want to remember him. I want to honor him by living a life of equal heroism and I want to call others to do the same. That's why I've written this book—to illuminate the heroic elements of Whitefield's life as a trumpet call to true greatness. The often-forgotten truth is that the lives of heroes past have a power of impartation, a grace to offer, as it were, to those willing to receive it. There is an ennobling in the contemplation of who they were, a confirmation of the truth that we become what we behold. That is why I've written this little book as I have, with its brief description of Whitefield's life, an examination of his heroic character, and a meditation on his enduring legacy. I have written in the hope that a new generation of Whitefields may run for God as men have never run before.

CHRONOLOGY

1714	Born December 16 in Gloucester, England.
1715	His father, Thomas, dies.
1722	Elizabeth, his mother, remarries, but the marriage is troubled and ends in 1728.
1732	Enrolls at Pembroke College, Oxford, working as a servitor to pay his tuition.
1733	Introduced to the Holy Club by Charles Wesley.
1735	Converted, seven weeks after Easter.
1736	Graduates from Pembroke, preaches his first sermon, and is ordained as a deacon in the Anglican Church.
1737	Whitefield's preaching electrifies Bristol and London.
1738	First voyage to America.
1739	Returns to England and is ordained a priest. Begins preaching in the open air to tens of thousands. In August sails for a second time to the American colonies.
1740	Whitefield's preaching sets the American colonies aflame.
1741	John Wesley attacks Calvinism. Whitefield responds.
1741	November 14: Marries Elizabeth James.
1744	John Whitefield, first son of George and Elizabeth, dies at four months.
1744–48	Third visit to the American colonies.
1748–51	Lady Huntingdon appoints Whitefield her chaplain.
1751	Fourth tour of the American colonies.
1752–54	Extensive ministry in Wales, Scotland, and London.
1754	Fifth trip to the American colonies. Receives an honorary M.A. from the College of New Jersey (now Princeton).
1755–63	Revival continues in England. Whitefield visits Holland to regain his health.

1763–65   Sixth tour of the American colonies.
1765–69   Continues revival work in England.
1768   Elizabeth dies.
1769–70   Seventh trip to the colonies.
1770   September 29: George Whitefield dies and is buried in
           Newburyport, Massachusetts.

Forgotten
Founding
Father

PART 1:
THE HEROIC LIFE OF
GEORGE WHITEFIELD

*"It is very easy talking what we can bear
and what we can do,
but let God lay his hand on us,
and we shall see what we are."* [1]

"We are immortal till our work is done." [2]

PROLOGUE

*T*HEY WERE going to die—hundreds of them. They were going to march through 350 miles of Canadian wilderness and give their lives to exhaustion, starvation, cold, and musket balls. Before they died they were going to get hungry, so hungry they'd eat boiled rawhide. Some would eat candles. A few would try to eat the Colonel's dog.

They would suffer through boiling rapids, chillingly steep ridges, and a series of accidents to make the most fearless patriot doubt his purpose. The unceasing rains would turn to snow and join the wind to punish as though for every sin of mankind. Always there would be the dead: dropping on the march, dying during the night, freezing at their posts. And ultimately, they would fail. They would not take Quebec. Nor would the reputation of their commander rescue them from their dishonor. Though once revered, he would show his true colors in time. His name was Benedict Arnold.

But none of this could they have known in September of 1775. All awaited them, concealed in the thickening fog of the future. What they did know was that the excitement of Lexington and Concord, of a few heady colonies tweaking the nose of the greatest empire in the world, had shattered against the harsh realities of war. They knew that many of their neighbors did not want a break with England and had no intention of joining the fight. They knew, too, that the British forces ridiculously outnumbered them, that even friendly nations were afraid to join their cause, that their merchant friends preferred selling to the British at a profit to provisioning the rebels at a loss, and that Congress seemed determined to do nothing but squabble.

All this they knew and yet they marched northward, a thousand volunteers from throughout the colonies, dreaming of better days and victories yet won. On September 16, a day they would never forget, they arrived at Newburyport, Massachusetts. Cheering crowds greeted them and refreshed their sagging spirits. The next day being Sunday, the officers decided to honor the kindness of the townspeople by parading the troops in general review. The pride and excitement were electric as the lines of soldiers marched up King Street—soon to be renamed Federal Street—with colors flying and drums rumbling fiercely. Suddenly, there were gasps and shouts of a different kind, for the crowd realized that the officers were marching their troops to a specific place—to Newburyport's beloved First Presbyterian Church.

As the delighted town folk proudly looked on, the soldiers marched through the door and up the main aisle of the church, formed two lines on either side, and presented arms. The drums maintained a steady roll. Chaplain Samuel Spring stepped forward and majestically walked between the lines of solemn soldiers to the pulpit. The men then stacked their weapons neatly in the aisle and filled the pews in quiet anticipation. Chaplain Spring looked down into the sea of faces, surely moved both by the moment and by the looming sense that many of these men would never enter a church again. It was time for him to speak. He chose his text carefully, from the words of Moses: "Lord, if your Spirit does not go with us, then do not send us." The men listened, nodding assent to every truth, filling the hymn that followed with heartfelt intensity.

It wasn't until afterward that someone realized where they were. This, after all, was not just any Presbyterian Church. In fact, this town was not just any town. Something special had happened here and just five years ago. It was then that the most famous man in the world, a man whom every colonist knew about and most had seen in person, came to this town and died. And while millions mourned him, the people of Newburyport buried him— right here, in the basement of the First Presbyterian Church, where he lay now under the feet of these worshipping warriors.

The news rippled throughout the command. Beneath where they were standing was the tomb of the man who had led the great revival from Georgia to New England. Tens of thousands had flocked to hear him as he roared the glories of the risen Christ. They had never been the same. Nor had he stopped with the subject of salvation. He had also spoken of God's purposes for the colonies, had called his American friends to return to the vision of their Puritan fathers. He had even warned the colonies of the encroaching control of a misguided Parliament. Hadn't he also been a friend of Dr. Franklin? Hadn't he converted some of the men who now led the revolution? Surely this man was as much the father of the movement as any. Surely a kind Providence had brought them to this place, this holy place, where now George Whitefield lay beneath their feet.

In an instant, they knew what they must do. With the sexton's permission, they went reverently below into the church's vault and found the tomb of the man some called "the apostle of the age." They stood silently for a moment, encircling the place where he lay. Then, gently, some of the officers opened the coffin. Five years' decay made the body unrecognizable, but they all remembered him. Some had seen him preaching in the open fields or had heard him in their churches. Others had read his sermons or given money for the orphanage he founded in Georgia or his school for Negroes in Philadelphia. Each of them had relatives whose lives were transformed by the preaching of this great man. He had made them one, had called them together as a people, and had turned them to their God. This revolution was as much his as anyone's. And now they were here.

They were moved, humbled. They wanted this holy moment to last and if it couldn't they wanted to take something of it with them. Someone pulled out a knife and gently cut off a piece of the collar or the cuffs that had survived the years. Others did as well. The sexton just watched, unable to deny them. The soldiers took the pieces of the preacher's garment and shared them among themselves. They tucked them in their boots or sewed them to their coats or put them in the lining of their hats.

But they kept them, and they kept them because they knew that the war they fought grew in large part from the truth he preached. He was their spiritual father, the man who called them to Christ and to Christ's purpose for their land. It was his vision of freedom for both soul and society that they now fought to defend. So when they marched out of Newburyport that day, they thought about what they carried and how much that godly man had done for them.

And when the cold came, and the hunger, when their friends died of disease or exploded in battle as though from within, they each remembered their little piece of the preacher's garment and drew from it a bit of the preacher's courageous heart for God. Thus the fires of revival spread into a blaze of freedom—and forged a nation in the process.[3]

A SEASON OF DARKNESS

*I*F IT is true, as Scripture teaches, that wickedness echoes in heaven—that the blood of Abel lifted its voice to God or that the outcry against Sodom and Gomorrah was heard above—then the sound that arose from eighteenth-century England must have made the angels weep. Though Charles Dickens wrote, "it was the epoch of belief, it was the epoch of incredulity, it was the season of Light, it was the season of Darkness," he was being optimistic.[4] Darkness definitely held the upper hand.

How surprising this is, though, given that not long before England had entered a golden age uniquely inspired by the glories of the Christian faith. Think of it: the English Bible of Tyndale, the English church of Elizabeth, the English state of Cromwell, and the English culture of Shakespeare, Milton, and Donne. Add to this some of the greatest theologians Christianity has ever produced and some of the most gifted artists in human history and it is not too much to wonder why England in the 1700's wasn't the shining star of Christendom.

But she wasn't. She was falling, hard, and it is difficult to know just why. It may have started in 1662 when an anti-Puritan Parliament ejected more than two thousand Puritan ministers from their pulpits. Or it may have begun when rationalism and her religious twin, Deism, transformed God into an absentee landlord, Jesus into a deluded fool, and the Bible into a collection of empty myths. Or it may have come on the wings of England's newfound prosperity, with all the soul-numbing entanglements of materialism in tow.

Whatever the cause, by the 1700's, England was a land of spreading spiritual darkness. Deism prevailed. Cynicism ruled. What passed for biblical faith was trotted out only on special occasions and then only to appease the unsophisticated masses. Prime Minister Robert Walpole knew the game well. When Queen Caroline was dying in 1737, he suggested to Princess Emily that the Archbishop should be summoned. The Princess hesitated. Walpole urged, "Pray, Madam, let this farce be played; the Archbishop will act it very well. You may bid him be as short as you will. It will do the Queen no hurt, no more than any good; it will satisfy all the good and wise fools, who will call us atheists if we don't profess to be as great fools as they are."[5]

As faith went, so went morals. Seldom in history has a nation changed its moral character so radically as England did in the late seventeenth and early eighteenth centuries. In the land where Puritans once ruled, Lady Montagu could quip that Parliament was "preparing a bill to have 'not' taken out of the Commandments and inserted in the Creed."[6] It was nearly true. Depravity had become the fashion, corruption the popular rage.

Vice ruled the day and bred a savagery that festered even in the law. The courts made more than 160 offenses, many of them minor, punishable by hanging. A new form of entertainment was born: the public execution. Crowds ridden with bloodlust jeered, taunted, and gambled on how long the victim would last. The wealthy enjoyed picnics in their carriages while listening to the last gasps of the dying.

It was a cruel and barbaric age. As evidence, bear baiting was a favorite attraction on city streets. Passersby stopped to watch while a man who had paid for the privilege beat a bound bear with a club. It was violent and angry, but then so were the people. Gangs ruled many neighborhoods and raging masses so often went on riotous looting sprees that they took for themselves the name "Sir Mob."

At the root of many evils was the national obsession with gin. In 1689, Parliament had forbidden the importation of liquor. It meant nothing. People of every class began to brew their own and soon England entered a horrible time called the "Gin Craze." Astoundingly, every sixth house in London became a gin shop with signs in "Gin Alley" advertising "Drunk for one penny, dead drunk for twopence, clean straw for nothing."[7] Often there was a price for dirty straw; customers comatose from drink wouldn't care. Gin solved everything. It was fed to infants when they cried, given to children to make them sleep, and consumed to the point of intoxication by most every adult. It poisoned men's souls, making them lazy, mean, and vile. One bishop complained, "Gin has made the English people what they never were before—cruel and inhuman."[8]

But this bishop, a Dr. Benson, was rare in the church of the day. Most clergymen nestled easily into the depravity of the age. When the French jurist and philosopher Montesquieu returned to France from England in 1731, he seriously reported that the English had no religion. "A converted minister," he concluded, "is as rare as a comet."[9] Clergymen spent their time foxhunting, drinking, gambling, and attending plays. When the Bishop of Chester chastised a priest for drunkenness, the man protested, "But my Lord, I was never drunk on duty!" "On duty," the bishop thundered, "pray, sir, when is a clergyman not on duty?" "True, my lord," stammered the priest, "I—er—never thought of that!"[10] King George II even found it necessary to remind the Archbishop of Canterbury, head of the Church of England, that his residence wasn't intended for gambling and whores.

Given the state of the church, the role of prophet fell to the nonbelieving. It was Lord Bolingbroke, certainly no friend of the faith, who pointed his finger at a gathering of priests and fumed, "Let me seriously tell you that the greatest miracle in the world is the subsistence of Christianity, and its continued preservation as a religion, when the preaching of it is committed to the care of such un-Christian men as you."[11] It was true, but a hard and drunken people could not hear.

So England descended. The church slept on. The rich grew distant and fat. Poverty spread like black death over the land. Africans were enslaved in increasing numbers. Children were worked to an early demise in factory and field. The innocent were hung or consigned to a living hell in rat-invested jails. Degenerate living filled the streets with urchins skilled at crime and addicted to vice. Illiteracy and ignorance prevailed and superstition arose in their shadow.

And where was deliverance to be found? Was it in the works of Addison or the eloquence of Burke or the statecraft of Walpole or Pitt? Was it in the satire of Johnson or Swift? Was it in a misguided church or a distracted Parliament? Was it in the grasping merchant class or the drunken, angry masses?

No.

Deliverance came from a public house in Gloucester. It came in the form of a fatherless, squint-eyed boy laughably named for the king of the realm. It came from one who later called himself "a worm taken from a public house."[12] But it came, and all because the wickedness of the age, and the prayers of the saints, reached to the heavens of a compassionate God.

A WORM TAKEN FROM A PUBLIC HOUSE

*O*N DECEMBER 16, 1714, a woman in the port city of Gloucester, England, gave birth to her seventh child. The delivery was a painful, tearing experience. The mother, whose name was Elizabeth, wouldn't heal fully for fourteen weeks—weeks of the kind of misery only a woman can know.

Still, Elizabeth was a creature of great depth and insight, the kind who pondered carefully everything she experienced. Lying in bed all those weeks with her little blue-eyed boy tucked contentedly at her side, she considered the manner of the child's birth. Slowly, it came to her. It had been a sign. This one was special, chosen for some purpose not yet revealed. It was God's way of making his will known. She knew it, as mothers always do, and she treasured the knowledge in her heart, not even daring to tell her husband. But one day, when the time was right, she would tell her little boy how special he was, how God had spoken so clearly in the way of his birth. So it was that on the day of Elizabeth's choosing, George Whitefield must have felt the first imprint of destiny upon his soul

Yet destiny fashions with many tools and it is not hard to find the signs of Providence in much of George's early life. It is deeply meaningful, for example, that he spent his early years at an inn. His father, Thomas, was the owner of Gloucester's Bell Inn, one of the finest in town, and it is easy to imagine how the odd assortment of people and their intriguing ways must have fascinated the little boy who moved almost invisibly among the distracted guests. That he grew up in Gloucester is also important, for the city was a bustling port with all the billowing sails and bustling docks one might expect. Whittling quietly on a busy wharf, George could see the massive clipper ships set to sea and the strange people of faraway lands, could hear the accents of the world. How these must have echoed in the dreams of a little boy's heart.

He was in many ways a completely normal child. He played the games of the neighborhood boys, teased his share of girls, and wasn't above stealing a sweet from a local stand or sneaking a peak through the window of the local bawdy house. More than anything he loved the dramatic. He read plays with delight and wormed his way into theaters whenever he could. He spent hours recreating what he had seen or read and he became so accomplished that he could often perform the Sunday sermons with greater effect than the original. Once when he was acting out a sermon for the entertainment of some guests at the Inn, he noticed some of them began to weep. It was a sign of what lay ahead, but

George was too young and too impressed with the attention to realize what was happening.

Despite his mischievous, dramatic flair, he also possessed a deeply religious nature. It was often confusing. He stole money from his mother's purse but then used it to buy religious books. He would fight viciously with boys in the streets and then fall weeping on the floor of his bedroom to pray for the souls of those he had just pummeled. His brothers and sisters thought he loved church just because it was a grand drama that suited his vain, theatrical little mind, but his mother later found him asking such astute questions that she knew something of the divine was penetrating his soul Sunday after Sunday. This, too, she treasured in her heart.

Some historians have suggested that both the theater and religion offered him escape, for George's early years were far from pleasant. In 1716, Thomas Whitefield died at the age of thirty-five. George was too young to understand at the time but the event had a profound impact on his life. Probably to find a father for her children and secure help in running the inn, Elizabeth agreed some time later to marry an ironmonger by the name of Capel Longden. It was a disastrous match. Anger and tension filled the home, which was only compounded by the mounting pressure of the inn, now declining under Longden's pitiful management. Finally, when he realized he couldn't wrest the inn from Elizabeth, Longden deserted the family and filed for divorcee. George was shattered both for the pain he saw in his mother's eyes and for the social stigma that divorce meant in the 1700's.

Eventually, George's older brothers took over the Inn and gave their lives to running it, but Elizabeth had other plans for her youngest child. Despite the pain of her broken marriage, she had never forgotten the signs of God's calling on George's life and she made arrangements for him to enter the school of the main cathedral in Gloucester, Saint Mary de Crypt. It was another signpost of destiny on George's path. The master of Saint Mary's was Daniel Bond, a wise and devoted teacher who immediately perceived George's gifts. Rather than discourage the interest his young scholars had in the stage, Bond fed their fire and even wrote plays for George and his friends to perform. With the skill of a true educator, he used their interest in theater to introduce them to the wider world of literature and ideas. He also helped them learn about themselves as they honed their dramatic skills and drew the admiration of Gloucester with their gifts. George thrived under Bond's care and never forgot the imprint of this skilled teacher upon his life.

Despite his rapid progress at Saint Mary's, George left the school at the age of fifteen. He later wrote that since his mother's "circumstances would not permit her to give me a University education, more learning I thought would spoil me for a tradesman."[13] It is a sad admission. He was, after all, descended from a long line of Oxford men and surely expected to attend the great university. Yet, because of his family's declining state, he decided to settle for the life of a tradesman. Returning to the work of the Inn, he became, he later wrote, "a professed and common drawer."[14] Still, the dream of Oxford burned in his heart. When he saw other young men setting off for school, it "cut me to the heart." When a friend from Oxford urged him to enroll, George could only sigh, "I wish I could."[15]

He had worked at the Inn less than a year when his mother, due to tensions in the family, decided to leave. George felt abandoned and soon found himself embroiled in the same problems that had driven his mother away. His brother, Richard, who now ran the business, had married and though it was arranged for George to become his assistant, he soon found that his new sister-in-law was a difficult creature to endure. He wrote later that the two could "by no means agree," that "at length the resentment grew to such a height, that my proud heart would scarce suffer me to speak to her for three weeks together."[16] George felt he was at fault and often went to his room to weep over his arrogance. Still, there was no peace and he determined to do as his mother had done and leave the inn.

It is not hard to imagine what a horrible time this must have been for him. His hope of attending Oxford was dashed. His mother, the one woman who sensed the higher meaning of his life, was forced away. He was even distanced from the family business through his own strife and foolishness.

Yet, here, even in this dark valley, destiny emerged. George went to be with another brother in Bristol. While there, he attended services at Saint John's Church. It was a life-changing experience: "I was carried out beyond myself. I felt great hungerings and thirstings after the blessed Sacrament, and wrote many letters to my mother, telling her I would never go into public employment again."[17] He turned his heart afresh to spiritual things and spent hours pouring over Thomas A'Kempis's *The Imitation of Christ*. He was "impatient till the bell rang to call me to tread the courts of the Lord's House."[18] It was an early quickening of the kind that often leads to true faith, but he sensed that somehow it would be short lived. Even "in the midst of these illuminations something surely whispered, 'This will not last.'"[19]

It didn't. Two months later he returned to Gloucester and fell in with his old crowd. He spent his time on plays and spent his money on pleasure. He knew he was far from God, far from the pursuit of his purpose, and it haunted him. In the unusual manner of those still in the world but coming to faith, he read his Bible and wrote sermons at night while living a life of sensuality during the day. His soul was ripped apart by the tension of his existence and he told his sister, almost as though to remind himself, "God intends something for me which we know not of."[20]

It must have seemed as though this confession moved the hand of God or perhaps that the hand of God moved the confession, for in no time an old schoolmate returned from Oxford and told George and his mother of how a poor student could go to the university as a servitor, serving other students to pay tuition. Elizabeth was ecstatic. "This will do for my son," she exclaimed. Then, turning to George, she asked. "Will you go to Oxford?" "With all my heart," he gushed and with Elizabeth seeking the help of wealthy friends who promised to secure admission when the time came, George returned to school to prepare for the dream of Oxford.[21]

Though he knew God had made a way, he couldn't bring himself to full repentance. He "continued in secret sin and at length got acquainted with such a set of debauched, abandoned, atheistical youths that if God by his free, unmerited, and especial grace, had not delivered me out of their hands, I should have long since sat in the scorner's chair. In short, I made great proficiency in the school of the Devil."[22]

Still, God did not abandon him, but gave him "such a distaste of their principles and practices" that he turned from the worldly ways of his former friends. He began to read Scripture and pray, to fast every Wednesday and Friday and to read religious books. He also studied his Greek New Testament and went to public worship twice a day. He did everything he thought religion meant, and he was sincere. He continued in this mode for a year and soon found that the friends he had once caroused with now followed him in godliness.

It was at this time, in his seventeenth year, that George had a dream, the first of many that would mark his path. He dreamed that he "was to see God on Mount Sinai, but was afraid to meet him."[23] What did it mean? He prayed and mulled it over and over. He couldn't let it go. Then, he shared it with an older woman whom he trusted. "George," she replied, "this is a call from God."[24]

THE LIFE OF GOD IN THE SOUL OF MAN

*I*N 1732, AT the age of eighteen and with the help of many Gloucester friends, George entered Oxford's Pembroke College. It was a thrilling moment. Almost immediately, though, there was work to be done. The servitor's work was waiting. His years at the Bell Inn now served him well. He would tend the laundry, clean the rooms, and serve the food of the wealthier students. Sometimes he would even do their schoolwork. With his spare time, he would attend his own studies and, hopefully, maintain his newfound religious regimen.

Not long before he came to Oxford he had come upon William Law's *A Serious Call to a Devout and Holy Life*. The book had a profound impact upon his soul. Law insisted that true godliness is evident in a "man who lives no longer to his own will, or the way and spirit of the world, but to the sole will of God, who considers God in every thing, who serves God in every thing, who makes all the parts of his common life, parts of piety, by doing every thing in the name of God and under such rules as are comfortable to his glory."[25] George got the message. Live by rule. Do every thing in every day for God. Waste nothing. Capture every moment and every task for the divine. Quickly, he organized his work as well as his devotion, praying, singing psalms, fasting, attending church, and studying Scripture all according to a prescribed routine.

During this time he heard of some men who were seeking to live much as he did. They were hated on the campus, filled as it was with wild parties and loose living. They met in a small group and encouraged each other in their faith. They even prayed well into the night and tended the wants of the needy. George watched them from afar. He heard them called "bible moths" and "methodists" because of their methodical devotion to holy living. Some even called them the "Holy Club," a name they kept for themselves. He watched as they walked to worship and were pelted with stones by a hateful crowd. He learned that their leader was a teacher at Christ College, just across the street from Pembroke, whose name was John Wesley. His brother, Charles, was also a member. George was too shy to approach them but when he heard of a poor woman who had attempted to cut her own throat, he sent word to Charles Wesley to see if he would help.

The story of this first contact is too tender to pass over. We can imagine George as an outsider who often walks alone in the woods about the campus. He is shy and insecure. He watches the Methodists from the edge of crowds, but never makes a move to join them. He looks for an opportunity, some excuse for connection. Then, one day, he learns of a poor woman's ghastly attempt at suicide. Suddenly, he has a plan. He finds an old apple-seller, a near institution at Oxford, named Apple Annie, and begs her to tell Charles Wesley of the desperate need but to be sure not to give his name. Apple Annie nervously approaches Wesley and tells him not only of the suicide but, we can imagine, of a young man at Pembroke who needs help, whose soul is tormented. Wesley remembers the lad, has seen him walking on campus. Apple Annie sheepishly returns to George with Wesley's invitation to breakfast the next day. What a sleepless night must have followed before that meeting that changed the world. Perhaps Apple Annie knew more than any gave her credit for.

The next day George met with Wesley and through him entered the Holy Club and the fellowship his soul longed for. He also entered the glories of Wesley's library. With Charles's encouragement, he read Francke's treatise *Against the Fear of Man* and a book entitled *The Country Parson's Advice to His Parishioners*. Then he found the book that changed his life: Scougal's *The Life of God in the Soul of Man*. We must realize that George had been trying to find true religion in the duties William Law suggested. Fasting, prayer, study, worship and every deed done for God were George's daily bread. But it hadn't filled him, hadn't given him the intimacy with the Father his heart desired. But here was Scougal, boldly declaring that "true religion was union of the soul with God, and Christ formed within us."[26] It was transforming: "a ray of

Divine light was instantaneously darted in upon my soul, and from that moment, but not till then, did I know that I must be a new creature."[27]

It was transforming, but not the ultimate transformation. He was too immersed in his doing, too given to duty as the path of holiness. He now sought to gain the life of God in his soul by living right, by leaving "no means unused, which I thought would lead me nearer to Jesus Christ."[28]

So began the season of extremes. George now tried to reach a higher goal by the same old methods newly energized. Once he fasted for days, now he fasted for weeks. He had always battled pride, but now he sought to break it by making sure everyone knew he was a Methodist, by going about campus unkempt, and by deliberately failing his classes. Not finding the deliverance he sought he became convinced he had a demon. He cried out for freedom, spending "whole days and weeks" lying prostrate on the ground in prayer. Something was wrong but he didn't know what. Perhaps he talked too much and God was displeased. Solution: don't talk at all. That didn't help? Perhaps he was too given to comfort. Solution: sit for hours in the snow. So it continued until people, including his friends, thought he was mad. A professor who saw George's work declining called him to his room and asked what was wrong. George burst into tears and could say no more. The professor concluded that the young man had simply lost his mind.

George couldn't help himself. He fasted until he couldn't walk up the stairs to his room and until other students asked, "What is his fasting come to now?" Doctors confined him to bed for seven weeks. Still his sins loomed before him: "All my former gross and notorious, and even my heart sins also, were now set home upon me, of which I wrote down some remembrance immediately, and confessed them before God morning and evening."[29] He spent two hours a day in his Greek Testament and in Bishop Hall's *Contemplations*. Still, his torment endured.

Then, deliverance, and in a most extraordinary way. "One day, perceiving an uncommon drought and a disagreeable clamminess in my mouth and using things to allay my thirst, but in vain, it was suggested to me that when Jesus Christ cried out, 'I thirst,' His sufferings were near at an end. Upon which, I cast myself down on the bed, crying out, 'I thirst! I thirst!' Soon after this, I found and felt in myself that I was delivered from the burden that had so heavily oppressed me. The spirit of mourning was taken from me, and I knew what it was truly to rejoice in God my Savior and, for some time, could not avoid singing psalms wherever I was: but my joy gradually became more settled, and, blessed be God, has abode and increased in my soul, saving a few casual intermissions, ever since. Now did the Spirit of God take possession of my soul, and, as I humbly hope, seal me unto the day of redemption."[30]

For the first time, he knew the life of God in the soul of man. He was free.

THE BOY PARSON

*W*ITH THE energy of the new birth just filling his soul, it so happened that George had to leave Oxford. He was simply too sick from his extreme disciplines. Besides, his money had run out. He returned to Gloucester for nine months, a season that proved an incubation period for his new life.

But he couldn't just rest. He was too excited about his fresh life in God. He first wrote all his friends and family about his experience. Then, he recovered the joy of spiritual disciplines. Rather than the legalistic duties he had once made his specialty, he now discovered that prayer, fasting, and study could be aflame with the Spirit. He read the Bible daily on his knees and it seemed that God was breathing through every page. He was full like never before and he longed for others to know what he knew. As he shared his new life with those he met, they, too, were converted. George formed them into Holy Club-like "societies" and pastored them as best he could.

Everything seemed new. He visited prisoners as he always had but now he reaped a harvest beyond his imagining. Prayer meetings and even giving to the poor seemed alive and powerful like never before. And, as he studied Scripture, "God was pleased to enlighten my soul, and bring me in the knowledge of His free grace and the necessity of being justified in His sight by faith only."[31] In short, he became a Calvinist, a man who believed in a sovereign God, the helplessness of men, and salvation as a free gift no man can earn.

It was about the time that he returned to Oxford with his health and finances replenished that he had another dream. He saw himself talking with a bishop in a palace and he saw the bishop give him some gold that seemed to make a sound in his hand. Not long after, the dream came true. Through the introduction of a friend, George found himself in the bishop's palace waiting for the Bishop himself. It was hard to believe. The bishop welcomed him and told him that he had heard of George's character, liked his behavior and had wondered at his age. He was twenty-one. The bishop had vowed he would not ordain anyone under twenty-three but told George that whenever he felt himself ready, he would ordain him. The bishop then gave George a handful of coins to buy a book and when the coins sounded in George's hand, he remembered his dream and his heart was "filled with a sense of God's love."[32]

Another man might have been elated by this experience. George was too conscientious, too aware of the weightiness. He was going to be ordained one day. He would have to stand in front of witnesses and answer the question, "Do you trust that you are inwardly moved by the Holy Ghost to take upon you this office and administration?" The very thought made him tremble. What would he say? Had he really felt called, truly been moved by the Holy Spirit to give his life to ministry? He didn't know, and a season of gnawing soul-searching and prayer ensued. It seemed a burden too great to endure.

Looking back on these days of agony some time later, Whitefield wrote, "I never prayed against any corruption, I think, in my life so much as I did against going into Holy Orders. I have prayed a thousand times until the sweat dropped from my face like rain, that God in His infinite mercy would not let me enter the Church *before he called me.* I remember once at Gloucester—I know the room, I look up at the window when I am there and walk along the street—I know the bedside and the floor where I prostrated myself and cried, 'Lord, I cannot go! I shall be puffed up with pride. I am unfit to preach in Thy great Name. Send me not, Lord; send me not yet.'"[33]

In time, though, he relented. Perhaps he truly received that inner confirmation of his call. Or perhaps he simply came to understand that few men enter ministry without doubts. Whatever the case, whatever his struggles, he finally submitted to what he came to see as the will of God. On Trinity Sunday of 1736, George Whitefield was ordained to preach the gospel of Jesus Christ.

The next week he preached his first sermon. It foreshadowed much that was to come. Three hundred of his closest friends, family, and fellow clergymen gathered in Saint Mary de Crypt at Gloucester, the church where he was baptized, went to school, and had his first communion. And what did they see? What kind of man stood before them in the pulpit of the grand cathedral? He was only twenty-one years old, of average height but thin from his excessive fasting. He had almost feminine features and a high forehead that gave the impression of a thinking, reflective man. Later, they would remember the eyes, small, dark-blue eyes that seemed to pierce their souls. They would remember, too, the unusual squint in one eye, the result of measles left untended by a family nurse when he was small. It could actually be endearing, though critics would later label him "Dr. Squintum" in a cruel attempt to paint him a religious clown.

As he mounted the pulpit to speak, the crowd took note of his stately bearing and how the robe and white wig seemed to speak of an inner nobility then just emerging. His voice, though, is what would never leave them. It was more a musical instrument skillfully played than simply a means of dispensing words. It was full, resonant, echoing. It had depth, range, and energy. It superseded his West Country accent, what some called a "twang through the nose" that made "Christ" come out as "Chroist." The quality of Whitefield's voice transformed the twang and made it piercingly beautiful. They would remember, those who heard him that first day in 1736, and so would thousands, indeed millions, afterward.

Yet, along with the voice they would always remember what followed. He spoke only a simple message about the need for Christian community. It lasted less than twenty minutes. But the crowd was electrified. Fifteen people became "drunk in the Spirit." Some said, "He preached like a lion."[34] Others complained and blamed George for the disorder of people undone in conviction. This "boy parson" had gone too far, they insisted. Still others rose to defend. Arguments ensued. The bishop watched closely, sensing a larger storm on the horizon. He was right. George Whitefield's first sermon told the whole story if people had only known how to read the signs.

Bishop Benson wanted to keep his gifted young clergyman close by and offered two small Gloucester parishes. George was honored but soon learned that influential friends urged the bishop to allow him to return to Oxford to pastor the Methodists there in the absence of the Wesleys, who were now in Georgia. The Bishop relented and, on the last day of June, George rode into Oxford to take up his duties.

He might have spent his entire life tending Methodist societies in the great university town, but a greater destiny awaited. A friend from the Holy Club invited him to take over his responsibilities for a month or two. Surely, the friend urged, some other Methodists can carry the load at Oxford while you replace me here for a season. George was dumbfounded, for the friend was Thomas Broughton, curate of the chapel at the Tower of London! It was every young man's dream to see London and every clergyman's dream to preach there and here was a chance for George to do both only weeks after his ordination. How God confirmed his way, George thought.

But fears settled in. London was a godless and unsympathetic place. It was one thing to preach in

Gloucester, his hometown, or to like-minded Methodists in Oxford, but London crowds were cynical and hard. It would not be easy. Almost before he knew it, he was there. His friends were thrilled to see him, but while walking down the street someone shouted "There's a boy parson" and it deflated him. Quickly he recovered and took the comment as an arrow of God to "mortify my pride."[35] Sensing the challenge he prepared himself even more zealously until the day of his first London sermon arrived.

It came on August 8. The people of the Bishopsgate parish—craftsmen, apprentices, shopkeepers, and prosperous merchants—waited at the start of the service, devout and bored. Then, a gasp from the back of the room and, in a moment, a giggle as a visiting pastor with a strange squint walked up the aisle. He mounted the pulpit but seemed dazed, perhaps awed by the size of the crowd. Clearing his throat nervously, he began and spoke on the new birth as though announcing the theme of a lifetime. The crowd barely moved but when he finished all knew something deep and transforming had taken place. There was a power beyond the human in his words, a feeling in the room that made faith arise and truth penetrate into the soul. Whitefield sensed the success of his sermon and slipped quickly out of the church once the service was over, hoping to escape any compliment that might feed his pride. People were left to ask each other who this young man was. No one knew, but word of his gifts spread.

For the next two months, George preached to crammed services every Sunday. The response was remarkable. His destiny had begun to overtake him and no one was more surprised than he was. He tried to escape the growing clamor by reading prayers in a nearby jail once a week and to the sailors on the nearby Wapping docks each evening. He hid away in his room in the mornings to study Scripture and his beloved *Matthew Henry Commentaries*. Still, his reputation for the pulpit spread and when his two-month assignment was finished people wept and pleaded to keep him from leaving.

He returned to Oxford but soon there was another request. His friend, Charles Kinchin, asked him to cover his parish at Dummer while Kinchin was away. Whitefield agreed. Probably he yearned for the solace that the rural parish of Dummer could provide. But when he arrived, he found that God intended further schooling for him. Rather than bring truth to an ignorant farm people, George found himself drinking deep from the simple yet profound lives in the little village. "The profit I reaped from . . . conversing with the poor country people was unspeakable. I frequently learned as much by an afternoon's visit as in a week's study."[36] The experience marked him, giving him not only a compassion for the poor, but an eagerness to honor men of every class and kind.

Yet Dummer marked him in another way, as well. It was while there that he decided to go to Georgia. He had already been contemplating his life's purpose and the meaning of these first blushes of success. While he reflected on these matters, a letter came from John Wesley. It spoke of the work in Georgia and the fields of harvest that awaited the bold and the willing. Wesley ended with the challenge, "What if thou art the man, Mr. Whitefield?"[37] The arrow hit its mark: "Upon reading it, my heart leaped within me, and, as it were, echoed to the call."[38] In an instant, it was done: George Whitefield was going to Georgia.

SETTING ENGLAND AFLAME

*O*N NEW YEAR'S DAY 1737, the fiery young preacher with visions of Georgia in his heart began one of the strangest and most glorious seasons of his life. Having announced his decision to go to America, he thought he would leave in a matter of weeks. In fact, he wouldn't sail for a year, the combination of weather and the schedule of George Oglethorpe, Georgia's founder, causing constant delay. Yet, in retrospect, the year was divinely ordained, for everywhere Whitefield went he lit the first brush fires of national revival—all during a time of almost unintentional ministry.

It began when he went to Gloucester to ask the blessing of the Bishop and to bid his family farewell. The first task went smoothly, for Bishop Benson blessed his young charge and said, prophetically, that Whitefield would "do much good abroad."[39] His family was another matter. They wept and bullied and enticed. He tore himself away but before he could leave a local priest asked him to preach, the tales of his successes in London having drifted back to Gloucester. He spoke twice to huge crowds while the "power of God attended the Word."[40] People wanted him to stay, but he went to Bristol to say good-bye to friends there and again received an invitation to preach. He did and the reaction was the same: surprise, power, conversions, crowds, and revival. The mayor of Bristol asked if he would preach before the city leaders. When he did, his sermon "made its way like lightning into the hearers' consciences."[41] Word spread and crowds thronged. The same thing happened at Bath and then at Oxford.

Almost uncomfortable with what was happening, Whitefield went to London to wait for General Oglethorpe before leaving for Georgia. More delays, though, and, thus, more ministry. He read prayers, preached, and met with the spiritually hungry. The fire of God attended his work: hearts melted, sinners repented, masses thronged his meetings. The pattern repeated itself for months in Gloucester, in Bristol, in Bath, back to London and then in all of them again. He would plan to leave, delays would intrude, and he would set hearts ablaze.

England had never seen anything like it. From every denomination, social class, and profession people came to hear the Word. Then, as Whitefield spoke, people would weep and shake violently, some even falling to the ground. Others screamed in terror as visions of a dark eternity loomed. Whitefield would continue on, unfazed. The chorus of weeping and travail and rapture grew louder. Finally, he finished in prayer and departed. There was never an altar call. He wanted true conversions, born of travail. To give those in grief of soul an easy path to relief made cheap the gospel. Let them linger in the pangs of the birth that made men new.

The attention Whitefield's preaching received was unparalleled: "The tide of popularity now began to run high. In a short time, I could no longer walk on foot as usual, but was constrained to go in a coach, from place to place, to avoid the hosannas of the multitude. They grew quite extravagant in their applauses; and, had it not been for my compassionate High Priest, popularity would have destroyed me. I used to plead with him to take me by the hand and lead me unhurt through this fiery furnace. He heard my request, and gave me to see the vanity of all commendations but His own."[42]

Feeding this amazing public ministry was an intensely powerful private life with God. "I found uncommon manifestations granted me from above. Early in the morning, at noonday, evening, and midnight, nay, all the day long, did the blessed Jesus visit and refresh my heart. Sometimes, as I was walking, my soul would make such sallies as though it would go out of the body. At other times, I would be so overpowered with a sense of God's infinite Majesty that I would be constrained to throw myself on the ground, and offer my soul as a blank in His hands, to write on it what He pleased."[43]

This devotion, combined with powerful preaching, allowed Whitefield to leap over denominational walls. Dissenters, those who had broken away from the Church of England, sensed Whitefield's sincerity, and told him "that if the doctrine of the new birth and justification by faith was preached powerfully in the Church, there would be but few dissenters in England."[44] Baptists, Presbyterians, and even Quakers sought his counsel, drawn by both the evidence of being truly born again and the faith of Jesus that Whitefield displayed. The makings of an inter-denominational revival were underway.

Finally, December of 1737 arrived along with word that General Oglethorpe's ship, the *Whittaker*, was about to sail. The previous twelve months had been astonishing. It had begun when Whitefield set out from the tiny village of Dummer heading for Georgia on New Year's day. It ended with the fires of revival raging and George Whitefield the most talked about man in England. He had been ordained barely eighteen months. How could it be? What could explain the thousands of awakened souls, the many Methodist societies, and the crowds, always the crowds? It must be simply the grace of God and his decision to use a slight, squint-eyed boy to change lives. What else, George might have wondered, did God intend?

The time to depart came. As Whitefield bid farewell to the crowds after each sermon, the outpouring of grief startled him. After one meeting, "I was nearly half-an-hour going out to the door. All ranks gave vent to their passions. Thousands and thousands of prayers were put up for me. They would run and stop me in the alleys, hug me in their arms, and follow me with wishful looks. Once in the Christmas before my departure, with many others, I spent a night in prayer and praise, and, in the morning, helped to administer the Sacrament at Saint Dunstan's, as I used to do on Saints' Days. But such a Sacrament I never before saw. The tears of the communicants mingled with the cup, and had not Jesus comforted our hearts, our parting would have almost been unsupportable."[45] Whitefield wasn't exaggerating. Charles Wesley, newly arrived from Georgia, was amazed at what he found and concluded, "The whole nation is in an uproar."[46]

Almost as Wesley spoke these words, the sails of the *Whittaker* filled with the winds that would carry her to America. The date was December 28, 1737. George Whitefield was twenty-three years old.

To Touch the Land of Destiny

NOW THERE came another delay. And a test. The *Whittaker* left London but soon discovered that strong southwesterly winds prevented her from sailing down the English Channel. As though doing the bidding of the grieving crowds, the weather itself conspired to keep Whitefield in England. For three weeks, the *Whittaker* anchored off Deal on the Kentish coast. As always, George Whitefield preached and, as always, people were set ablaze for God.

During this frustrating but fruitful time, a note came from John Wesley who had just returned from Georgia. It had not gone well. His ministry had failed, a love affair with a young woman had ended painfully, and legal charges against him had almost landed him in jail. What is more, Wesley was yet unconverted, his famous "strangely warmed" experience at Aldersgate yet several weeks in the future. He was, in short, a broken man.

But he had heard from God for Whitefield, he claimed. Wesley believed in receiving divine guidance by casting lots, which meant putting possible answers to a problem on small sheets of paper and drawing them at random out of a hat. He had done this to receive guidance for White-field's trip to Georgia. The answer? "Let him return to London." God had spoken, Wesley believed, and sent a note to his friend on the *Whittaker*. George was shaken. Had he missed God? Was he going in presumption? He had such respect for Wesley, such confidence in his integrity and spiritual clarity. He cried out to God, searching for the light to know his path. Soon, peace came and the assurance he needed. He later wrote, "I knew that my call was to Georgia and that I had taken leave of London."[47]

It was a test and Whitefield passed it. There was a great deal in the balance. Luke Tyerman, among the most renowned of Whitefield biographers, has written, "Who can estimate what would have been the consequences of Whitefield's yielding to Wesley's wish? Had he returned to London the probability is he would never again have started for America; and, in such a case, many of the brightest chapters of his history could never have been penned."[48] We can go further than this. Had White-field never gone to America, the great revival there might never have happened. And, had there been no great revival, there may well have been no American Revolution. The consequences of the decision to go, despite Wesley's revelation, were huge.

He arrived at Savannah, Georgia, on May 7 to find a situation of ministerial devastation. The fact is the

Wesleys had left a mess. John Wesley, as yet unchanged of heart by the new birth, was as rigid and unyielding a missionary as any on record. He had insisted that colonists of every persuasion conform to Anglican ritual, refused to admit the sale of rum, maintained an icy distance from the common folk, fell into a disastrous love affair with the Chief Magistrate's daughter and left the colony under indictment by a grand jury. The colonists were scandalized, yet when Whitefield arrived, he chose a higher tone: "I think it prudent not to repeat grievances."[49] Rather than dwell on past failings, he set out to win the Georgians—whom he was warned were "full of devils"—and soon found that "America is not so horrid a place as it is represented to be."[50]

It was hot, though. That was true. The heat boiled the feet and steamed the air into a suffocating wool blanket of wetness. There were mosquitoes and Indians and rude accommodations. But Whitefield was a Methodist, a man inured to hardship. After falling sick briefly, he began ministering the Word to the colonists and was thrilled with what he found: "They hear the Word gladly and are not angry when I reprove them . . . I have endeavored to let my gentleness be known among them because they consist of different nations and opinions: and I have striven to draw them by the cords of love because the obedience resulting from that principle, I take to be most genuine and lasting."[51]

As always, he gave himself to a whirlwind of activity, ministering tirelessly to soldiers, his "red coat parishioners" whom he had come to love on shipboard. He arranged for the building of a church, tended congregations in Savannah and Frederica, and endeared himself to the Italian, German, Dutch, French, and Indian members of the English colony. He also set himself to care for the growing number of orphans in Georgia.

The colony had been founded as a place for debtors to work off their outstanding accounts. The laws of England imprisoned a man for debt but gave him no way to earn what he owed. George Oglethorpe, much influenced by the Methodist devotion to prisoners, petitioned the crown for permission to start a colony where debtors could work to pay off their debts and build a prosperous future.

The idea was good but the going was hard. Men died in the cruel wilderness of the New World and some, showing the character that landed them in prison to begin with, simply abandoned their commitments, including their children, and fled. The colony was swarming with orphans and the sight touched Whitefield's heart. He decided an orphanage had to be built and that he was the man to do it. Having won the approval of the colony's leaders, he had only to gain approval back in England and then begin raising funds. It was a small step, perhaps, but the decision placed enormous burdens on Whitefield for the rest of his life.

At the end of four months, it was time for him to return to England. He had not planned to stay long on this first voyage anyway and the time had come for him to be ordained as a priest. His previous ordination had been as a deacon, the first of a two-stage process required by the church. Besides, the vision of the orphanage burned within him and the money to build lay in England. Still, he left with regret, for America, his "little foreign cure," spoke of a promise and destiny that touched his heart. He loved the freedom, the rough people, the possibilities, and the sense of divine purpose that permeated the land. Vowing to return, he sailed for England on August 28, 1738.

THE MAD TRICK

$\mathcal{W}$HEN WHITEFIELD arrived in England on November 30th, he found the situation there far different from when he left. The Wesleys had experienced the new birth, which had lifted them out of a narrow and deadly form of legalism into the broad, sunlit pastures of salvation by grace. They almost immediately became the leaders of the revival Whitefield had started and through powerful preaching and organizational gifts, the movement spread quickly. The doctrines of the new birth were preached from the greatest pulpits of the land, from Saint Mary's at Oxford to Westminster in London. Converts were organized into societies, hymnbooks were published, and churches were set aflame by the Spirit.

Sadly, success bred opposition. Leading clergymen raged against the message of the new birth and resistance within the church closed pulpits to the Methodists. Whitefield returned to find that doors previously opened were shut and that the nation once described as in an "uproar" because of his preaching was now in an uproar of a different kind.

There was more. During his voyage to America, Whitefield had written reports intended for his Methodist friends only. Penned in a style familiar to his spiritual circle, with all the airy phrases and ethereal language that people of common faith tend to use. They were not intended for publication, but they were published and without Whitefield's knowledge. While the public loved them, the clergy were incensed. Whitefield seemed to be bragging about his impressions from God, the size of his crowds, and the favor he received from officials. He appeared extreme, unstable, and arrogant. Critics of the revival used these impressions against him and Whitefield found he moved under a cloud of suspicion as he returned from America.

The situation was dire but there was hope. The two Wesleys and Whitefield met with other friends and "mused until the fire burned." They talked, prayed, encouraged, and planned. "About three in the morning," Charles Wesley wrote, "as we were continuing instant in prayer the power of God came mightily upon us, inasmuch that many cried out of exceeding joy, and many fell to the ground. As soon as we were recovered a little from that awe and amazement at the presence of His Majesty, we broke out with one voice, 'We praise Thee, O God! We acknowledge Thee to be the Lord!'" It seemed a commissioning, a confirmation they were indeed God's people fighting God's battles in God's due season. They left with "the conviction that God was about to do great things."[52]

But matters grew worse. Critics circulated a pamphlet calling Whitefield a peddler of strange doctrines and a menace to order in the church. Eager not to nurture bitterness, Whitefield took the pamphlet to his room, fell to his knees and prayed for the author. Then there was the incident at Saint Margaret's. Whitefield arrived at the famous church to find that another man had been asked to preach, though a large crowd had gathered at word of Whitefield's appearance. Whitefield deferred, offering to leave the pulpit to the other man, but members of the congregation resisted. He told them to solve the matter themselves while he enjoyed the service, now halfway through. Before long, an usher showed him the way to the pulpit and Whitefield assumed the matter had been decided. He preached, the crowd was deeply affected, and he thought the matter was finished. He awoke the next day to find that he was being called a pulpit stealer and rumors were circulating that he had physically prevented the rightful preacher from fulfilling his duty. The stories weren't true, but they were damaging and many pulpits closed to him afterward. His only response was to remark that opposition "brings me nearer to my master."[53]

These trials proved a great benefit to the work of revival, though, for they gave rise to Whitefield's "mad notion." It all started at Kingswood, where he had long yearned to preach to the coal miners and their families. The depravity of these people was legendary. They lived in shacks and were reputed to be gin-devils, wife beaters, sodomites, and thieves. They perfectly illustrated Thomas Hobbes's famous description: "No arts; no letters; no society; and which is worst of all, continual fear and danger of violent death; and the life of man, solitary, poor, nasty, brutish and short."[54]

The plan had been forming in Whitefield's mind for some time. The pulpits of the land were closing to him rapidly, but the people were hungrier, more responsive, than ever. What should he do? Somewhere he had heard of preachers in Scotland, perhaps in the Highlands, preaching out of doors. It was unheard of in his day, though he had almost done it once or twice himself. He had refrained. It just wasn't done. But now, as he heard of these poor people the mayor of Kingswood called "Indians," he knew the hour had come.

On Saturday, February 17, 1739, George Whitefield stood on a little hill in Kingswood, England, and lifted his voice. The coal miners must have thought him insane. There he was, a twenty-four-year-old parson, in robe and wig, holding a prayer book and preaching aloud from the gospel of Matthew. But something was strange. They could hear his voice, that amazing voice, a hundred yards away. The crowd gathered. They had never seen the like before. In fact, most of them had never seen a preacher before.

And this one was different: he opened his sermon with a joke, told stories they could understand, and made invisible truths real to the eyes of the heart. Hundreds had gathered, their coal-blackened faces peering back quizzically at the young preacher. He continued, not knowing what to make of their silence. Then he noticed something. There were white streaks appearing on the faces. Could it be? Yes, the miners were weeping.

Repentance followed and soon laughing and singing. Their hearts had melted before the Word and not just a few but hundreds. It became known as the Kingswood Revival and soon the whole nation marveled at the works of God among the hardest hearts of the land.

George Whitefield was changed that day. He had experienced a kind of deliverance, a liberation from men's opinions, from the idol of respectability, from his own fears. Already a man on a mission, now he had a method to match his call. A new boldness filled him and he declared, "My preaching in the fields may displease some timorous, bigoted men, but I am thoroughly persuaded it pleases God, and why should I fear anything else?"[55]

It was good that he had such a sense of divine pleasure, for the clergy raged anew. Pulpits closed, denunciations filled the press, and threats of excommunication flew like arrows from the bow. Even some of the Methodists doubted the wisdom of such a tactic. The young evangelist didn't care: "Field preaching is my plan; in this I am carried as on eagles' wings."[56]

The freedom of field preaching enflamed his soul. He discovered a flow of spiritual power like he had never known. He preached again in Kingswood and this time to thousands instead of hundreds. The meetings continued, night after night, and the crowds grew. Typically, Whitefield discovered the coal miners' need for a school and began to raise money for it. He asked them also to remember the orphans of Georgia and these poor people of the forest gave more than they could afford. Whitefield was undone. How he loved these people and how thankful he was that their needs moved him to

embrace field preaching as the means of reaching a
nation bound by darkness.

Finally, the great climax arrived. It was Sunday,
March 25, when more than twenty-three thousand
people gathered to hear the young preacher's final
sermon. Standing upon his makeshift pulpit, Whitefield
looked out and saw "the open firmament above me, the
prospect of the adjacent fields, with the sight of thousands and thousands, some in coaches, some on horseback, and some in trees, and at times all affected and
drenched in tears together, to which sometimes was
added the solemnity of the approaching evening, was
almost too much for, and quite overcame, me."[57] After
Kingswood, Whitefield was never the same.

His weapons now were loaded and his target clearly
in view: London. There, in the chief city of the land, he
would step into the parks and public places to call the
masses to his God. No narrow-minded priest, no bigoted
bishop could keep him from fulfilling the call of God. It
was time for the true faith to step from the shadows into
the light of midday. Let the enemy be on the run. Whitefield was on the move.

It began at Moorfields, a public park filled with enter-
tainment-seeking crowds. The meeting was small but
clearly anointed, Whitefield thought. No one stopped him
and the words flowed freely. He then preached at Kennington Common, a twenty-acre park where executions
often drew large crowds. Standing by a permanent scaffold, he spoke of the certainty of death and the horrors of
hell. The crowd that gathered was huge. Indeed, Whitefield reported that it was as much as thirty thousand,

most of whom seemed deeply convicted, weeping and screaming their repentance.[58] The sight filled him with fresh vision. He preached at Moorfields and Kennington again and again, adding from time to time a new location, like Hampstead Heath or Bedford.

During these days, he began a practice that became his pattern for life. He called it "preach and return." He would preach at a new location with the intent of plowing the ground and sowing the seed of the Word. But then he left and wouldn't return for a while. He wanted the seeds to grow, the Word to spread like leaven. He then returned when he sensed the time was right and his schedule allowed. He was usually overjoyed to find the disciples multiplied, the wickedness of the place dramatically reduced, and the people hungry for more.

His second series of meetings were most always a huge success and the momentum allowed him to take two important steps. First, he formed the masses into societies or small groups to nurture Christian growth. Second, he raised the vision for some good work which the people were encouraged to support—the feeding of the poor, the building of a school, and meeting the ever-present needs of the orphans of Georgia. He did this because he wanted more than just revival: he wanted a spiritual revolution, a transformation of society by the power and truth of God's kingdom.

For those living in London during the summer of 1739, it must have seemed that revolution had already come. Everywhere Whitefield spoke the crowds were gigantic, the conviction was deep, and the city was changed by the good works and holy living of the faithful.

It is hard to understand from this distance the enormity of what was happening. At one sermon in Hyde Park, more than eighty thousand people gathered to hear him.[59] Even allowing for exaggeration, that number "leaves a staggering total, a crowd the size of which had not been seen in all England since the great battles of the Civil War."[60] In fact, during those amazing summer months in London, Whitefield preached to somewhere between eight hundred thousand and a million people. It was more than any Englishman had ever addressed in the entire history of the nation.[61] It surely seemed that all England was destined for awakening and, as always, the Pharisees of the age lifted their voices in a chorus of protest. Yet, as one biographer has poetically written, "the more his enemies roared, the more his popularity soared."[62]

The meetings continued, dozens of them: at Cirencester, Tewkesbury, Bristol, Basingstoke, Rodborough, Stroud, and Hampton Common. He even found himself preaching in a field that adjoined the Bell Inn at Gloucester. What thoughts must have crossed his mind. Did he think of those difficult early days under the heavy hand of his stepfather? Did he remember telling his sister that God intended something special for his life? Did he think back to his childhood sins and the dreariness of work in a tavern? We cannot know. Yet, surely we can imagine the gratitude and the awe he felt when he preached next to his childhood home having become, at twenty-four, the most famous man in English history, a leading light of the most astonishing spiritual movement ever to flood the land.

It was time to return to America, though. The work of the orphanage called and the beckoning promise that cities in the northern colonies—Philadelphia, New York and Boston—might ignite as London had. So it was that on October 30, 1739, Whitefield arrived at Lewes, Delaware, almost exactly a year after his last departure from American shores. But he was a different man and now he had a different dream.

He had begun to see it in London, with the fires of revival blazing around him. It then grew clearer during the weeks at sea. God wanted an international revival, a complete spiritual renewal of the entire English-speaking world. Wasn't it obvious? Times had changed. A consumer revolution was happening, with all the transportation, trade, communications, and intercolonial connections that an empire grasping for riches demanded. God intended to use these ready-made connections, and the marketplace mentality they produced, to spread the gospel like never before. There was going to be a nation-transforming revival, growing on the back of the consumer revolution, and George Whitefield was the man to set it in motion.

TO MAKE A PEOPLE ONE

*T*O LAUNCH the American version of the dream, Whitefield chose Philadelphia, then the largest city in the nation. It began on November 6. He read prayers and preached at Christ Church to a "numerous congregation." The people were moved and pleaded for more. The moment had come. As one historian has written, "he moved out of doors and the revival was on."[63] Two days, later, he preached to more than six thousand people—nearly half the population of the city.[64]

The story of the Philadelphia revival can best be told by one who was there: Benjamin Franklin. When he first heard Whitefield, Franklin was thirty-three years of age. He had come to Philadelphia nineteen years before, ragged and poverty-stricken, but soon became a successful printer, publisher, alderman, and magistrate, destined to be one of the most influential of American statesmen. Franklin was fascinated with Whitefield. He took note that "the multitudes of all sects and denominations that attended his sermons were enormous," but he also marveled at the changed lives. "It was wonderful to see the change soon made in the manner of our inhabitants. From being thoughtless or indifferent about religion, it seemed as if all the world were growing religious, so that one could not walk through the town in an evening without hearing psalms sung in different families of every street."[65]

Ever the man of science, Franklin determined to measure the extent of Whitefield's amazing voice. He walked off an imaginary line from the courthouse steps where Whitefield spoke, down to Market Street and all the way to Front Street by the river. "Imagining then a semi-circle," Franklin reported, "of which my distance should be the radius, and that it were filled with auditors, to each of whom I allowed two square feet, I computed that he might well be heard by more than thirty thousand. This reconciled me to the newspaper accounts of his having preached to twenty-five thousand people in the fields, and to the ancient histories of generals haranguing whole armies, of which I had sometimes doubted."[66]

But Philadelphia was only the beginning. Whitefield set his face to preach northward to New York. On the way, he met William Tennent and his son, Gilbert, who had just begun a "log college" at Neshaminy. The elder Tennent was "an old grey-headed disciple and soldier of Jesus Christ" who stormed out his sermons in a most fiery, prophetic way. Whitefield loved him immediately and preached in his little log school, one day to become Princeton University.

In New York, Whitefield met with miraculous success. Some have suggested that this was in large part due to the absence of theater in the colonies. Americans had heard preaching, but they had never seen the divine drama that Whitefield offered. Thousands gathered and were never the same. The Rev. Ebenezer Pemberton, later the minister of New York's Presbyterian Church, recorded what the huge crowds saw: "All he said was demonstrative life and power. He has a most ready memory, and, I think, speaks entirely without notes. He has a clear and musical voice, and a wonderful command of it. He uses much gesture but with great propriety. Every accent of his voice, every motion of his body *speaks*; and both are natural and unaffected."[67] Clearly, Whitefield was the best show in town, but it was a show with eternal consequences.

He used his gifts not only to reach individual sinners, but to pull down the strongholds of religious pride and division. In an oft-repeated sermon, Whitefield pretends he is talking to Abraham in heaven.

"Father Abraham," he cries. "Whom have you in Heaven? Any Episcopalians?"

"No!"

"Any Presbyterians?"

"No!"

"Any Independents or seceders, New Sides or Old Sides, any Methodists?"

"No! No! No!"

"Whom have you there, then, Father Abraham?"

"We don't know those names here! All who are here are *Christians*—believers in Christ, men who have overcome by the blood of the Lamb and the Word of his testimony."

"Oh is that the case? Then God help me, God help us all, to forget having names and to become Christians in deed and in truth."

It was vintage Whitefield and whole towns were changed by its strength.

Returning now to the Philadelphia area, he preached in Elizabeth Town, New Brunswick, Maidenhead, and again in Neshaminy. He wrote John Wesley, "Do you ask what I am doing? I answer 'ranging and hunting in the American woods after poor sinners.'"[68] When he returned to Philadelphia on November 24, the storm of revival broke out once again. Thousands tearfully attended his meetings. Even the Quakers of the city were moved, for Whitefield, tapping into their passion for Jesus, loved them, welcomed them, and involved them in the great work of revival. When he announced he was leaving the city, the outcry was beyond belief. On November 29, the day of his departure, people thronged his door, crying and pleading, at seven in the morning. A company of two hundred horsemen escorted him from the city and the justices, who were in session, suspended their business until he had preached his final sermon. No like honor had ever been given before.

He rode south by horseback, preaching through Maryland, Virginia, and the Carolinas. He met huge crowds that were truly remarkable given the distances people had to travel in the rural south, but he was repulsed by the stench of slavery in the land. Whitefield is a bit confusing on this point, because he was not opposed to slavery completely. He thought Scripture permitted it and actually encouraged it in Georgia. But he was furious at how slaves were treated. He saw slavery as a means of evangelism and economic progress, but in the South he found a slavery more cruel and inhuman than he had ever dreamed and it tore at him. He told some that he was "sensibly touched with a fellow-feeling for the miseries of the poor Negroes."[69] This was after his first exposure to the bondage of Africans. In time, he understood how bad it could be and wrote an open letter to slaveholders chastising them for their heartlessness and inhumanity. It did not endear him in the southern colonies.

It was about the time that George reached his beloved Georgia, ending his preaching tour for a time and turning his attention to the needs of the orphanage, that a truly odd incident occurred in his life. He proposed marriage. He had long been enamored of one Elizabeth Delamotte, whom he first met in 1737 when he had been a guest in the Delamotte home. Elizabeth was a known beauty and Whitefield was already a celebrity. There was clearly an attraction. Almost immediately his journals began to include confessions of "inner trials" and "wrestling with the flesh." It must have meant further torment that he sailed to America on a ship named *Elizabeth*. But his problem was not just whether to marry this woman, but whether to marry at all. Methodism had not prepared him for love and pleasure. It was austere, other worldly, ever looking for some fleshly enjoyment to sacrifice. Whitefield himself referred to marriage as "a falling by the hand of a woman." He had even urged groups of single women with a sermon called *Christ, the Best Husband*.

But he came to realize he was in love, or something like it, and in 1740 he wrote to Elizabeth to propose marriage. His letter is almost pitiful in its attempt to propose what Whitefield wasn't sure he wanted. Luke Tyerman, one of Whitefield's early biographers, wrote that the great evangelist was "as odd a wooer as ever wooed."[70] It was true. In his proposal, he filled the first paragraph with a list of all the hardships the wife of a preacher would endure. Warming to his point, he told her, "I have great reason to believe it is the divine will that I should alter my condition, and have often thought that you [were] the person appointed for me." That was as close to a confession of love as he got.

He then assured her that he was free of the "passionate expressions" the carnal use and that he thought "ought to be avoided by those that would marry in the Lord." Then, the conclusion: "If you think marriage will be in any way prejudicial to your better part, be so kind as to send me a denial. I would not be a snare to you for the world. I trust, I love you only for God, and desire to be joined to you only by His command and for his sake." Historians usually conclude that Elizabeth was put off by such a tepid statement of affection and her parents were unwilling for her to bury herself in the woods of Georgia. In either case, four months later Whitefield received a letter that amounted to a rejection. He would later find that another man had entered Elizabeth's life and it would break his heart. Speaking of the biblical story of Jacob and Rachel, he confessed to a friend, "I was called upon to sacrifice my Rachel."[71]

With the proposal to Elizabeth and the business of the orphanage behind him for a time, Whitefield now turned toward New England. He was about to experience some of the greatest success of his ministry. He quickly made his way to Boston, having sailed first to Rhode Island, and there found many pulpits closed to him. As always, he simply moved out of doors. He preached to thousands on Boston Common and nearly eight thousand at Thomas Foxcroft's Old Brick Church, one of the few to welcome him.

Boston was a city of seventeen thousand and it wasn't long before nearly all of them had heard the young preacher. Many didn't have any choice. His almost supernatural voice carried down the cobblestone streets and echoed off the brick walls of New England's finest city. Whitefield preached his simple but dramatic message about the ravages of sin, the horrors of hell, the wonders of God's love, and the glories of salvation in Christ. The crowds, many descended from the great Puritan fathers of New England, were deeply convicted and turned again to the God of their fathers. Whitefield thought it a sign: "Surely the Lord intends to put the whole world in a Flame."[72]

With Boston astir, Whitefield began to preach to the surrounding towns. He preached in concentric circles around the main city, as he had in London and Philadelphia, using his standard "preach and return" strategy. As was his pattern, he preached two sermons a day in the most public place possible and spent as much time as he could meeting with seekers and "awakened" clergy. It was exhausting. In eight days he traveled 178 miles by horseback and preached sixteen times. He became ill, vomited repeatedly and often went to bed between sermons. Still, he found that when he stood in the pulpit, "the power of the Word" took over.

While touring Massachusetts, Whitefield was invited to preach at Northampton in the church of the famed Jonathan Edwards. Already revival had come to the western town as Edwards preached sermons like his trademark *Sinners in the Hands of an Angry God*. When Whitefield arrived, there was great excitement, many believing that even greater signs of God's mercy would come to the town in the wake of his preaching. The people enjoyed four sermons by the famous young preacher and while there is no record of what Whitefield preached, his *Journals* show he remembered the experience well: "I began with fear and trembling, but God assisted me. Few eyes were dry in the assembly. I had an affecting prospect of the glories of the upper world, and was enabled to speak with some degree of pathos. It seemed as if a time of refreshing was come from the presence of the Lord."[73]

Jonathan and Sarah Edwards were as touched as any by the power of Whitefield's ministry. Jonathan reported that he felt "weak in body" and wept the entire length of each sermon. Sarah was equally touched and later wrote a remarkably insightful letter to her brother, telling of her impressions of Whitefield: "He makes less of the doctrines than our American preachers generally do," she reflected, "and aims more at affecting the heart. He is a born orator. It is wonderful to see what a spell he casts over an audience by proclaiming the simplest truths of the Bible. I have seen upwards of a thousand people hang on his words with breathless silence, broken only by an occasional half-suppressed sob . . . A prejudiced person, I know, might say that this is all theatrical artifice and display; but not so will anyone think who has seen and known him."[74]

For his part, Whitefield admired Sarah Edwards for being "adorned with a meek and quiet spirit." He reflected on what it would be like to have a woman of such caliber. Clearly, he was thinking of Elizabeth.

Whitefield continued to preach throughout New England, finding particular success in Connecticut. In fact, it is from the pen of a Connecticut farmer that we have one of the most moving testimonials of Whitefield's fame and preaching power. In Middletown, Nathan Cole tended his farm and pondered carefully the amazing revival stories that came his way. How he longed to hear the "grand itinerant" for himself. Then, Cole heard that Whitefield was coming to Middletown. We know that more than four thousand people attended that meeting and it was long remembered. Cole himself was there, was deeply touched, and went home afterward to write down what he experienced. It is a moving testament to Whitefield's impact in the American colonies.

Here, in part, is Cole's account:

> Now it pleased God to send Mr. Whitefield into this land; and my hearing of his preaching at Philadelphia, like one of the old apostles, and many thousands flocking to hear him preach the Gospel, and great numbers were converted to Christ, I felt the Spirit of

God drawing me by conviction; I longed to see and hear him and wished he would come this way . . .

Then on a sudden, in the morning about 8 or 9 of the clock there came a messenger and said Mr. Whitefield preached at Hartford and Wethersfield yesterday and is to preach at Middletown this morning at ten of the clock. I was in my field at work. I dropped my tool that I had in my hand and ran home to my wife, telling her to make ready quickly to go and hear Mr. Whitefield preach at Middletown, then ran to my pasture for my horse with all my might, fearing that I should be too late.

Having my horse, I with my wife soon mounted the horse and went forward as fast as I thought the horse could bear; and when my horse got much out of breath, I would get down and put my wife on the saddle and bid her ride as fast as she could and not stop or slack for me except I bade her, and so I would run until I was much out of breath and then mount my horse again, and so I did several times to favour my horse.

And when we came within about half a mile or a mile of the road that comes down from Hartford, Wethersfield, and Stepney to Middletown, on high land I saw before me a cloud of fog arising. I first thought it came from the great river, but as I came nearer the road I heard a noise of horses' feet coming down the road, and this cloud was a cloud of dust made by the horses' feet.

It arose some rods into the air over the tops of hills and trees; and when I came within about 20 rods of the road, I could see men and horses slipping along in the cloud like shadows, and as I drew nearer it seemed like a steady stream of horses and their riders, scarcely a horse more than his length behind another, all of a lather and foam with sweat, their breath rolling out of their nostrils every jump. Every horse seemed to go with all his might to carry his rider to hear news from heaven for the saving of souls. It made me tremble to see the sight, how the world was in a struggle.

I found a vacancy between two horses to slip in mine . . . When I saw Mr. Whitefield come upon the scaffold, he looked almost angelical; a young, slim, slender youth, before some thousands of people with a bold undaunted countenance. And my hearing how God was with him everywhere as he came along, it solemnized my mind and put me into a trembling fear before he began to preach; for he looked as if he was clothed with authority from the Great God, and a sweet solemn solemnity sat upon his brow, and my hearing him preach gave me a heart wound. By God's blessing, my old foundation was broken up, and I saw that my righteousness would not save me.[75]

It was a scene repeated thousands of times and not just in the fledgling towns of America, but in the cramped cities of England, the vast pastures of Scotland, and the rolling hills of Ireland. Whitefield was truly the most famous, the most sought after, and the most influential man in the English-speaking world.

Yet, his impact upon New England was singular. He had read the Puritan writings and he sensed that New England had forgotten her God and his hand in their origins. When he preached to the sons and daughters of "the first comers," he reminded them of a destiny, a calling, that made the exploits of their ancestors possible. After preaching to tens of thousands of New Englanders in more than 175 sermons, he left not only awakened individuals but also a revived vision of corporate purpose that caused people to view their world differently. In time, this new perspective would infect all of the colonies. Later men would remember these times and know that the Spirit of '76 was conceived in the revivals of decades before. Whitefield had some sense of this, for he summarized his American tour by confessing, "All things concur to convince me that America is to be my chief scene for action."[76]

DAYS OF STRIFE AND TORMENT

RESH FROM victories in America, Whitefield
returned to England in February of 1741 and
found himself in a firestorm. There were two causes.
First, some letters in which he attacked a famous archbishop had reached the press. Second, John Wesley had
decided to "print and preach" against predestination in
general and Whitefield in particular. Whitefield reported
that "the world was angry at me for the former and numbers of my own spiritual children for the latter."[77]

The attack by Wesley was the most painful. Whitefield had known for some time that he and his friend disagreed on the issue of predestination, but he never
dreamed that it would come between them. The cause of
revival was too great, the cause of Christian liberty too
dear. But Wesley could not let the matter rest and had
drawn lots to know God's mind. His lot told him to "print
and preach," so, while Whitefield was in America,
Wesley began preaching against predestination. He also

printed a sermon entitled *Free Grace* that painted White-field's doctrines in such hellish terms that many saved in the revival began to wonder if the man who led them to Jesus wasn't a heretic.

Wesley feared that Calvinism, the idea that God chooses who should be saved and draws them by his own power, was a veiled version of fatalism. If God determines who is saved, why preach the gospel? In fact, why even bother with holiness if heaven is assured already? Besides, who could love a God who chose some for salvation by his mercy but chose others for hell? Where was the mercy in that?

Whitefield responded that Wesley's God was too small. Would so great a God leave salvation in the hands of fallen men? Does the Bible really teach that God provided salvation through his Son but left sinful men to find it on their own? No, he roared. God is an all-powerful God who chose from before creation who should be saved and who should not. It is his mercy that any are saved at all and those who are receive it as a free gift and then honor their Savior by living in holiness and spreading the news of his love. After all, Whitefield urged, God promised that seed time and harvest time would never end, but men must still sow and reap. So it is with preaching the gospel. God uses the foolishness of preaching to save the lost, but salvation is his doing.

Had there been more grace, less pride, and a higher cause in view, this might have come to no more than a loving disagreement among brothers. As it was, the revival was ripped in two. At times, it was vicious. Wesley printed his *Free Grace* sermon in America, which brought Whitefield into question there. Whitefield, on the other hand, mounted the pulpit in Wesley's church, the Foundery, and preached predestination as the truth of God. Offense reigned. Congregations split, church doors slammed shut, and believers parted company forever.

Whitefield was heartbroken that "many of my spiritual children, who at my last departure from England would have plucked out their own eyes to give them to me, are so prejudiced by the dear Messrs. Wesleys' dressing up the doctrine of Election in such horrible colors, that they will neither hear, see nor give me the least assistance."[78] Instead, many of his converts sent "threatening letters that God will speedily destroy me."[79]

In time, tempers cooled and the two men reached an "agreement to differ," but the movement was never again unified. Wesley's "United Societies" grew separately from Whitefield's "Calvinistic Methodist" groups and the cause of both revival and Christian unity suffered. Not until Whitefield gave up formal leadership of the Calvinistic Methodists in 1749 did he cease to pose a threat to Wesley and thus open the door to greater cooperation. The dispute wrote a dark chapter in the pages of church history. Had Whitefield's evangelistic fire and Wesley's organizational genius never parted ways, the Great Awakening may well have been greater still.

Devastated by his break with Wesley, bruised by attacks in the press, and scarred by the hatred of his former converts, Whitefield now had to face even greater opposition than before. The heckling at his meetings became violent. He wrote in his journal, "I was honored with having a few stones, dirt, rotten eggs and pieces of dead cats thrown at me." At one meeting a man tried to stab him to death. At another, opponents hired a drummer to drown him out. He was beaten, his pulpits were smashed, and on several occasions cattle were driven through his audiences. He even preached one sermon while a man tried to urinate on him.

Heated opposition attended him the rest of his life. Once, he was nearly murdered. After a long day of preaching, Whitefield retired one evening only to be awakened by word that a man had come to see him. The weary evangelist agreed to see him and in a few moments a young gentleman was sitting in his room. "Do you know me?" the man asked. "No," Whitefield replied, when instantly the visitor jumped up and began beating Whitefield with his gold-headed cane while screaming "Dog! Rogue! Villain!" Covering his head with his hands, Whitefield shouted, "Murder! Murder!" Soon, the landlady and her daughter were screaming for help as well, which only brought a second man who told the first, "Take courage, I am ready to help you!" The sound of help arriving drove the two assailants off. Whitefield appeared unhurt and tried to comfort the two women. Later, people remembered that he returned to bed murmuring the words from the Anglican Litany, "From murder and sudden death, good Lord deliver us."[80]

Recalling this incident, he later wrote, "I received many blows and wounds; one was particularly large, and near my temples. I though of Stephen, and was in hopes, like him, to go off in this bloody triumph to the immediate presence of my Master."[81]

Sometimes Whitefield's attackers suffered more than their victim did. Once when he was riding to a meeting with another man, a robber met them on the road and demanded all their money. The cocked pistol in his hand was argument enough and the two did as the robber insisted. The robber left and the two continued on. In a few moments, the robber returned and demanded Whitefield's coat, saying, "It is better than mine." The preacher did as he was told and the thief threw his old coat to Whitefield and rode away again.

As Whitefield and his friend continued on their journey, they looked behind them only to see the robber riding at full gallop toward them again. Deciding enough was enough, the two spurred their horses and reached the next town safely before the robber reached them. Later they wondered why the thief tried to get to them a third time, but when Whitefield felt the lining of the thief's coat, he found the answer: inside was a purse with many times more money in it than the thief had taken. The thief had apparently realized his error and sought to get his coat back. It was too late. The money went to the orphans of Georgia.

It was during this time of turmoil and struggle that Whitefield decided to marry—and to yet a second Elizabeth. It came about oddly. Whitefield's friend, Howell Harris, had fallen in love with a woman named Elizabeth James but had decided that he wanted "no creature between my soul and God."[82] Knowing of Whitefield's desire to marry, Howell hit upon a solution. He would introduce Elizabeth to George, thus removing himself from temptation. He arranged a meeting of the two and when Elizabeth discovered the motive she was furious. "If you were my own father you had no right of disposing me against my will," she protested.

Still, she seemed interested. He definitely was and proposed marriage four days later. She agreed and the two were married a few weeks after with Howell Harris giving the bride away. During the weeklong honeymoon, George preached twice a day. Within two months he was writing, "O for that blessed time when we shall neither marry nor be given in marriage, but be as the angels of God."[83] Historians have long debated how happy the marriage was and what it meant to Whitefield. It is hard to know, but there is evidence of times of joy between the long absences. Elizabeth died in 1768 and George grieved her, telling friends he felt lost without her.

The Methodist attitude toward marriage, though, could not have served them well. Most of Whitefield's fellow leaders saw it as a distraction from their calling and grieved a friend's marriage as they would his death. A comment by one Methodist hints at the state of the Whitefield marriage and well describes the attitude of many at the time. "Matrimony has quite maimed poor Charles Wesley," he wrote, "and might have spoiled John [Wesley] and George [Whitefield] if a wise Master had not graciously sent them a brace of ferrets."[84]

Not long after marrying Elizabeth, Whitefield experienced one of his most fruitful seasons of ministry. The high point was at Camberslang in Scotland. Revival had continued in the small village since some of its ministers had attended Whitefield's meetings at Glasgow years before. The leaders at Camberslang begged Whitefield to come and finally he agreed.

In a letter to Elizabeth, he told the story of the revival still revered in Scotland until this day. "I preached at two to a vast body of people," he wrote, "and at six in the evening and again at nine at night. Such a commotion surely never was heard of, especially at eleven at night. It far outdid all that I ever saw in America. For about an hour and a half there was such weeping, so many falling into deep distress and expressing it in various ways, as is inexpressible . . . Their cries and agonies are exceedingly affecting." He couldn't get the sound of it out of his mind: "All night in the fields could be heard the voice of prayer."[85]

Using his preach and return strategy, Whitefield left and returned a week later. He preached to nearly twenty thousand people who seemed electrified by the power of God. Communion services followed with Whitefield, an Anglican priest, serving Presbyterian congregations the body and blood of Jesus. One of the ministers serving with him noticed that he "appeared to be so filled with the love of God as to be in a kind of transport."[86]

Week after week, he preached throughout Scotland, fanning the flames of what could only be described as a Scottish Great Awakening. When he returned to Camberslang for another Communion service, forty thousand stood in the rain to hear him preach. The whole nation seemed enthralled with the power of God. A generation later, the revival was still touching lives. Whitefield knew something astounding had happened, but tried to keep perspective. "The work seems to spread more and more," he wrote a colleague, "O my friend, pray and give praise on behalf of the most unworthy wretch that was ever employed in the dear Redeemer's service."[87]

A few months after the Camberslang revival, Elizabeth announced she was pregnant. George was ecstatic. As fathers often do, he began planning the child's future, deciding instantly it would be a boy and he would be an evangelist. In fact, the boy's name would be John, for George saw himself as a Zacharias to his own Elizabeth. It was an exciting time. George left Elizabeth at the Bell Inn and ministered for months in England and parts of Wales. He planned to be there at the birth, but Elizabeth delivered early. George was away on an evangelistic tour, as usual. "The last evening of it I preached from a balcony to many thousands, who stood in the street as comfortable as at noon-day. Upon retiring to my lodgings, news was brought me that God had given me a son."[88]

George rushed home, baptized the child before a large crowd and then left for another tour. On the evening of February 8, 1744, he returned to the Bell Inn excited to see Elizabeth and his son. His older brother met him, white-faced and miserable. Then he saw his mother, weeping uncontrollably. The child had died after only four months of life. George was devastated. He had hoped for so much and now the child was gone. What could he do? He comforted his wife, buried the child and, returned to his preaching. "Weeping," he insisted, "must not hinder sowing."[89]

KINGDOM ON THE MARCH

*W*ITH THE death of their child fresh on their hearts, the Whitefields left for America in 1744. It was a horrible crossing, taking almost twelve tumultuous weeks and nearly killing them in a mid-sea collision. George went ashore so ill that people feared his death. He always recovered in preaching, though, and soon found strength to feed the still-lively fires of revival. There was much good news. Revivals had increased both in number and power since his last visit. In fact, the revival was changing the colonies, bringing them together and giving them a common vision. People spoke of "glorious gales of the Spirit" and wondered, with Jonathan Edwards, if the great revival of the days before Jesus' return was already upon them.

Whitefield preached with as much power as ever, but his health was failing. He vomited great amounts of blood after preaching, suffered horrible pains of angina, and spent sleepless nights with chills and "the flux." Fellow ministers begged him to rest, but he couldn't stop. He was desperate to spread the same kind of revival in America as he had known in Camberslang. He sensed, too, that mighty changes were on the horizon in America and that time was running out. He had to finish the work, raise up the leaders, and fulfill his duty to his beloved America.

He preached from Boston to Savannah and arrived at the orphanage in fall of 1745. From its small beginning, the orphanage had grown into the lynchpin of the whole weak and struggling colony. Visitors took note of the beautiful gardens, happy children, and excellently furnished buildings. But always there were burdens of debt and labor and to relieve both he made a decision that became what some have called his "black spot," he decided to buy slaves.

Though he had chastised southern slaveholders for callous treatment of their Negroes, Whitefield did not believe that slavery was immoral. He, like most Christians of his time, saw nothing in Scripture that prevented it and had become convinced that it might even be a tool of reaching a lost race. Besides, he needed the labor if the orphanage was to survive and Africans withstood the blistering Georgia heat better than white workers did. The first slave he ever owned was a gift from a friend. He purchased others in time and eventually even argued for the legalization of slavery in Georgia. It seems a contradiction of his otherwise compassionate nature but the record does show that he was kind and gentle to his slaves and that some, when freed, preferred to stay in his service. One historian notes "His slaves were the best treated, the happiest in the entire South; he even brought out a young man to look after their spiritual and temporal interest."[90] Still, Whitefield's acceptance of slavery has been called, "The one dark blot upon an otherwise unspotted character."[91]

He returned to England in 1748 with yet another successful American preaching tour behind him. As soon as he arrived, he received an invitation from the Countess of Huntingdon to preach in her London drawing room. Lady Huntingdon was an amazing woman of deep faith and courage who had come to embrace Methodism through the influence of her two sisters-in-law, both of whom had married Methodist preachers. She supported the movement generously and defended it valiantly. Tales of her boldness were legendary. When Bishop Benson told her that he "bitterly lamented" ever ordaining Whitefield, the Countess replied, "Mark my words, when you come upon your dying bed, that will be one of the few ordinations you will reflect upon with complacence."[92] It was as she prophesied. From his deathbed, the old man sent Whitefield a message of encouragement and a gift of ten guineas.

His ministry had been among millions of the common folk, but now Countess Huntingdon opened the door for Whitefield to touch the lives of the rich and the powerful. He preached in her home to a gathering of nobles such as the Viscount Bolingbroke and Lord Chesterfield. The human heart being what it is, both rich and poor, the Word of God had much impact. People wept and yielded to the power of Whitefield's words. Then, they asked him to speak again. It was the beginning of a broader work of the Spirit among England's ruling class.

The openness of upper class hearts to Whitefield's messages raised many an eyebrow. Lord Chesterfield's wife, the half sister of George II, was one of them. When King George saw her at court, wearing a pretty gown that was still much plainer than those of the other ladies attending, he approached her and said, "I know who chose that gown for you—Mr. Whitefield! And I hear you have attended on him this year and a half." Lady Chesterfield held her own. "Yes, I have," she replied, "and like him very well." Some scoffed, but many were intrigued that one among the "despised Methodists" should reach even to the court of the King. When courtiers urged him to restrain Whitefield, the King joked, "I believe the best way will be to make a bishop of him."[93]

Many of the nobles and wealthy of the land secretly admired Whitefield but couldn't muster the courage to withstand the ire of their peers if they acknowledged him publicly. Some, like Nicodemus approaching Jesus, sought out Whitefield privately. Lord Chesterfield was among them and when he found the man who had so moved him, he said, "Sir, I will not tell you what I shall tell others, how I approve of you."[94] Lady Huntingdon went further. She made Whitefield her chaplain, an honor he bore in addition to his degree from Oxford and his ordination. Now, when his name appeared in print, it included the words, "Chaplain to the Right Honorable the Countess of Huntingdon."

Whitefield's popularity among the ruling class sealed what was already an astounding level of fame.

Some historians conclude that he had spoken to more people than anyone else in human history. Yet, it wasn't just his speaking ability that made him so effective in shaping lives. It is Whitefield the evangelist who is best known, but Whitefield the strategic builder, the publishing phenomenon, and the philanthropist played their role as well.

After his successful crusades in the heart of London, Whitefield began building churches to disciple his eager converts. He built a "Tabernacle" at Moorfields which at first was little more than an ugly shed, but in 1753 was rebuilt to seat thousands in comfort. He also built a church at Tottenham Court Road where tremendous revivals took place under the preaching young ministers Whitefield had discipled. But there were more. In Bristol he built a meeting place at Kingswood, site of the great revival among the coal miners, and another at Penn Street. At Gloucester, there were three more. Today, there are still churches on most of these sites, the children and grandchildren of the ones Whitefield built, having survived the ravages of both wars and modernization.

Aside from this network of churches, it is important to remember that Whitefield was astonishingly influential as an author and publisher. His sermons were among the most widely read literature of the age in both England and the American colonies. With his *Journals* he virtually invented a new style of literature, one that was personal, even conversational, rather than in the formal, stilted style of the day. Many do not know that he took over a magazine called *The Weekly History* and used it to spread news of the revivals. And to counter the influence of what he called "bad books," Whitefield entered into numerous deals to have books he deemed important printed, often with his introductions included and often at such a price that the masses could afford them. Many books were brought back into print which would not otherwise have seen the light of day in Whitefield's generation, all because he knew his converts needed them.

Publishers clamored for his business. Even opponents of the revival worked to get rights to his projects, sometimes daring to print his sermons alongside editorials critical of his message. He was simply big business. In fact, Benjamin Franklin, who rejected Whitefield's message while still admiring him, became a wealthy man in part because of his rights to the American editions of Whitefield's printing projects.

There were also his projects to help the poor. Along with Bethesda in Georgia he tried to fund a school for Negroes in Philadelphia. Always he was raising funds, for a school here, a feeding program there, or perhaps for a community center that would double as a church in the town that could afford neither. We must remember that Whitefield raised thousands of pounds for these projects at a time when most clergymen lived on fixed salaries and could barely keep their churches in repair given the meager offerings they received. The simple truth is that Whitefield invented the business of ministry and did so with a purity of heart that those of the same business would do well to remember today.

To Free the Land of Promise

*H*E WAS famous, he was effective, and he was tired. He had spent years rushing from nation to nation, city to city, and he was wearing out. Crowds that had once seen a slim young man of energy and fight now saw a heavy, white-haired man who moved clumsily and breathed out his sermons with effort. Still, the power was there, that transforming energy that attended his words.

Men tried to build monuments to his work and put his name on the buildings of institutions he had pioneered, but he would have none of it. "No, let the name of Whitefield die," he wrote, "so that the cause of Jesus Christ may live. I have had enough popularity to be sick of it."[95]

Amazingly, he continued in his last decades as he had in his first. There were more tours of the American colonies, more foraging in Scotland and Wales, and the constant pattern of "preach and return" throughout England. He kept up the pace despite declining health.

Friends often urged him to go to bed rather than preach. He would refuse, need help mounting the pulpit, and then, feeling the familiar presence, would preach as men had come to expect.

Yet, it was in these last weary years that he again shaped the history of the world. His beloved American colonies were stirring with a new sense of purpose, a purpose that had largely grown from the revivals he led. When he first began preaching there, the colonies were little more than isolated settlements hugging the coastal regions, more connected to England than to each other. They differed widely from each other. Some were Quaker, some were Puritan, others were Catholic or Anglican. Making matters worse, they were separated by treacherous wilderness and equally daunting differences of culture.

That was before the Great Awakening. As George Whitefield began preaching from Georgia to Massachusetts, the colonies became one. Whitefield was, as one historian has written, the "first inter-colonial event." Newspapers followed the news of revivals in distant colonies as though they were in the next town. For the first time, the American colonists had a common experience that gave them a sense of corporate life they had never had before.

But it was more than just a social experience. Whitefield's preaching turned the colonists to a God many had long forgotten. The result was holiness, generosity, and a new devotion to the person of Jesus. Yet, there was more. He called them to see themselves in terms of a divine destiny, as part of the outworking of God's plan for the nations. This gave them a new identity, particularly as he reminded them of their Puritan heritage and the dream of becoming a "City upon a hill," a Christian light to all men. On the wings of these truths arose a new identity, an American identity, forged in the fires of the great revival.

It was an awakened, inspired people, then, that Parliament offended with new taxes to pay the bills of the French and Indian Wars. It was a people with a unique sense of corporate purpose who found their complaints ignored, their goods destroyed, their homes invaded by soldiers, and their legislatures treated with spite. Inevitably, there was going to be a conflict between the first determined strides of a newly awakened land and the grasping demands of a crumbling empire. It would ultimately lead to revolution and no one saw it more clearly than George Whitefield.

It is a story that has seldom been told. Whitefield was more than just the preacher who brought the colonies together before the great day of independence. He was in many ways an encouraging elder brother to the fledgling independence movement, a gentle hand tending the first sprigs of liberty.

It began with a warning. In 1768, six students were expelled from Edmund Hall at Oxford because they practiced "extempore prayer." Whitefield was furious. The expulsions were intended to wipe out Methodists and the very kind of practices that grew from the revivals. But Whitefield saw more in it. Only a few months before, the church had issued a document insisting that no missionaries would be sent to America except "such as have had a literary Education and have been bred up with a design to dedicate themselves to the Ministry."[96] Whitefield understood what this meant. Only Anglicans would qualify under such a requirement. English Christians of other persuasions would never be allowed to share their faith in the New World. And, more, Whitefield knew that there had long been an attempt to plant an Anglican bishop in the colonies. This would make the colonies Anglican when Whitefield knew that they were far more diverse, far more awakened and free, than an Anglican bishop would ever allow.

So he sounded the alarm. He wrote a letter, published on both sides of the Atlantic, charging that the Anglican Church was more interested in spreading its influence than in spreading the gospel. He warned his American friends that plans had long been laid to place a bishop in the colonies and that events in England meant that day wasn't far off. Leaders in America, like Samuel Adams, heard the alarm and repeated it throughout the colonies, making religious issues as much a cause of hostilities as the oft cited "taxation without representation."

Whitefield's support of the American cause took many forms. He championed the colonial case against the Stamp Act, accompanied Benjamin Franklin to Parliament to make American grievances known, and heatedly defended the colonial cause to British leaders. Equally important, he increasingly merged political and spiritual themes in his sermons.[97] He spoke often of liberty and the obligations of church and state to preserve it. Writing in his journal, he once tellingly asserted, "Religion is likely to go on well when both civil and ecclesiastical powers are engaged in keeping up the purity of it."[98] With such statements he helped the colonists envision a new kind of government, one distinct from the church in function but equally given to the cause of true faith. It was a dream as old as Augustine and Calvin, but George Whitefield made it part of the American dream, a gift succeeding generations of Americans ought to remember with lasting honor.

The Fading of the Light

*J*UST AS the American star was ascending, White-field's own light was growing dim. In 1770, he was fifty-six years old, but worn beyond his years. He was glad to be touring America once again, the land he now called his "home." He had preached throughout the colonies and found himself, late in the year, returning to New England. His health was worsening and many tear-fully recognized that they were seeing him for the last time.

He frequently said that "sudden death is sudden glory" and those who traveled with him had seen him often near the end.[99] In September of 1770, his passing seemed assured. Every day he grew weaker, wheezing and coughing through the night while barely able to walk during the day. Still he preached. Still, the power came. But the time seemed at hand. As he rode out of Portsmouth, New Hampshire, on a Saturday morning, a friend remarked, "Sir, you are more fit to go to bed than to preach." Whitefield replied, "True, sir," and then looking up to heaven he said, "Lord Jesus, I am weary in thy work, but not of thy work. If I have not yet finished my course, let me go and speak for thee once more in the fields, seal thy truth, and come home and die."[100] Later that day, he preached for two hours in the fields. His text was 2 Corinthians 13:5: "Examine yourselves to see whether you are in the faith."

It was a strain, though. An eyewitness remembered the scene: "He rose from his seat, and stood erect. His appearance alone was a powerful sermon. The thinness of his visage, the paleness of his countenance, the evident struggling of the heavenly spark in a decayed body for utterance, were all deeply interesting; the spirit was willing, but the flesh was dying. In this situation he remained several minutes, unable to speak. He then said: 'I will wait for the gracious assistance of God, for he will, I am certain, assist me once more to speak in his name.'"[101] He then preached, by all accounts, one of the best sermons of his life.

But he was spent. He dined with a friend afterward, rode to Newburyport, Massachusetts, and made his way to the house of a local pastor. Some remembered later that a crowd gathered in the yard when news of his arrival spread. They wanted a sermon. Whitefield was reluctant, but he mounted the stairs toward his room, stopped halfway, and told the pastor to let the crowd come in. He gave a short exhortation and when the candle in his hand burned to its socket, he finished and retired to his room.

Some time later, a fit of asthma seized him. He asked his friend, Richard Smith, to open the window. Then, he sat up in bed, coughing and wheezing, barely able to breathe. Smith later remembered that Whitefield began to pray. He reminded God of the churches in England, of the tabernacles at Moorfields and Tottenham Court Road. In spirit he crossed to Georgia and Bethesda, then to Pennsylvania and New England.[102] He was handing over his life's work. He finished. Time passed without a sound. Finally, looking up to Smith, he said simply, "I am dying."

It was five in the morning, September 30, 1770. For an hour he struggled for breath, going to the window for air, returning again. It did not help. At six o'clock, he groaned his last breath and entered the "sudden glory" of his dreams.

HE WAS buried at Newburyport, in the Presbyterian church where he had often preached. There was mourning, in Massachusetts and around the world. Funeral orations filled the cathedrals of the English-speaking world. In slave quarters and Indian huts, at sea and in the squares of a thousand cities and towns, news of his passing filled the air with weeping the like of which had not been heard since Whitefield preached the good news of God's love.

Yet some gave a higher tribute. A sailmaker in Portsmouth named Benjamin Randall had heard Whitefield . . . and hated him. At noon on the day of the great preacher's death, the town crier went about Portsmouth shouting, "Whitefield is dead. Whitefield is dead." The words thundered into Randall's soul. Falling to his knees, he cried aloud "Whitefield is dead, Whitefield is in heaven, but I am on the road to hell." Shaken, the young man yielded his heart to God where he knelt.[103] In time, he would preach the gospel himself and launch the Free-Will Baptist movement. But on that day, September 30, 1770, he was but a first answer to Whitefield's lifelong prayer:

> *Let the name of Whitefield die,*
> *That the cause of Jesus Christ may live.*

Part 2:
The Heroic Character of
George Whitefield

"The sun hath its spots, and so have the best of men." [1]

"I have put my soul, as a blank, into the hands of Jesus Christ my Redeemer, and desired him to write upon it what he pleases. I know it will be his own image." [2]

PREACHING

"That reformation which is brought about by a coercive power, will be only outward and superficial; but that which is done by the force of God's Word, will be inward and lasting. Lord, make me meet by Thy grace for such a work, and then send me." [3]

*I*T CAME to be known as the famous "Thunderstorm Sermon" and those sitting in the Boston meeting house never forgot it. It was classic Whitefield. The great preacher mounted the pulpit and prayed the usual opening prayer; usual except that some said "he seemed to kneel at the throne of Jehovah and to beseech in agony for his fellow beings."

As he began the sermon, storm clouds moved in, darkening the tall glass windows of the church. Then, the sun again and shadows played on the walls before the darkness returned. Whitefield seized the moment: "See that emblem of human life! It passed for a moment and concealed the brightness of heaven from our view. But it is gone! And where will you be, my hearers, when your lives are passed away like that dark cloud?"

Soon the church grew darker still, as the rumble of thunder drew near. Whitefield continued, painting the wrath of God in horrible hues, facing each soul with its place in eternity.

Then, a shattering spike of lightning.

"See there! It is a glance from the angry eye of Jehovah!"

Whitefield paused, the tension at breaking point. Thunder roared, leaving a horrible echo in the room. People jumped, some whimpered.

"It is the voice of the Almighty as he passed by in his anger!" he roared.

A tremendous crash. The storm unleashed its full fury. Whitefield covered his face with his hands and fell to his knees in silent prayer. The people in the pews were riveted with fear and held tightly to their loved ones.

Then came quiet, the passing of the storm. A rainbow appeared. Whitefield rose. "Look upon the rainbow," he whispered so all could hear, "and praise him who made it. Very beautiful it is in the brightness thereof. It compasseth the heavens about with glory, and the hands of the Most High have bended it." In a few moments he had finished and the people scurried home, thankful to have survived.

As Whitefield walked out of the church, someone approached and asked if he had any objection to the sermon's publication. "No," he replied, "if you will print the lightning, thunder, and rainbow!"[4]

It was a masterpiece and it was all men had come to expect from George Whitefield. The greatest actor of the day, David Garrick, once admitted, "I would give a hundred guineas if I could say 'Oh!' like Mr. Whitefield."[5] It was said he could move people to tears simply by the way he said "Mesopotamia."

He had loved the stage since childhood, enjoying a reputation for his mimicry and his memory for dialogue. But when he experienced the new birth, something dormant awakened in his soul. He found grandeur of expression flowing through him, an inspired ability to make his words paint rich tapestries of meaning in the minds of his hearers. His passion for Jesus, his love of God's word, and his gift for expression merged to produce sermons that were indeed anointed works of art. He became the finest preacher of his age, one of the greatest in history. For Whitefield it was simple: "I preach as a dying man to dying men."[6]

And, indeed, much of Whitefield's preaching success did come as the fruit of passion. He gave himself to the flow of "religious feeling" and often wept as he spoke. Some criticized him for it. "You blame me for weeping," he responded, "but how can I help it when you will not weep for yourselves, though your immortal souls are on the verge of destruction?"[7] But there was more. He knelt and gestured and enacted dramas from the Scriptures. He preached his doctrine through the symbols of everyday life, pointing at a tool in the hand of a listening farmer or using some truth about crops or how birds fly to make his point. The people understood as they never had before.

Much of this success was possible for Whitefield because he had learned to preach without notes, an astonishing break from tradition at the time. Most clergymen read their sermons, often failing to make eye contact with their audiences during the entire time they spoke. In fact, most clergymen were learned men who quoted lengthy passages of Greek or Hebrew, not to mention the German and French which were common in biblical scholarship, but which they never bothered to translate for their barely literate audiences.

Whitefield was appalled: "I think the ministers preaching almost universally by note, is a mark that they have, in a great measure, lost the old spirit of preaching. Though all are not to be condemned who use notes, yet it is a symptom of the decay of religion, when reading sermons becomes fashionable where extempore preaching did once almost universally prevail."[8]

Whitefield's sermons were so powerful he didn't even have to preach them for lives to be changed. When mimics repeated his lectures to entertain tavern customers, people were converted on the spot. In fact, the grace of God so attended his words he often saw fruit when he thought he had failed: "I have often found that my seemingly less powerful discourses have been much owned by God."[9]

The sermon had been entombed as a religious art form when Whitefield arrived on the scene. He rescued it. He made it what it ought to have been all along: a desperate plea to a perishing people, a confrontation with the word of the living God. In fact, to say that Whitefield was a great preacher almost diminishes him. Preaching was never an end in itself. It is closer to the truth to say that Whitefield was a great lover of men or a fiery intercessor before God. Preaching was merely the way his heart reached out to the lost and the hurting. It is why people were so deeply affected and why so many thousands were able to say, as one listener did, he "gave me a heart wound."[10]

ANOINTING

"Oh, how Divine truths make their own way,
when attended by Divine power!" [11]

*I*T WAS almost always there. Sometimes it wasn't. When it was, the words flowed, the ideas were clear, hearts were opened, and lives were changed. When it wasn't, all was strain and push and disappointment. It was what Jesus had and the early church prayed for. Giants like Augustine and Luther, Spurgeon and Moody, knew they were nothing without it. For lack of it, mighty men have wept like children and felt themselves abandoned by God. With it, the weak and the simple have changed whole nations.

It was the anointing of God and George Whitefield knew he was nothing without it. When he stood to preach, he waited for it, sometimes continuing in silence for quite some time though thousands looked on. As it came, he began to speak. He was familiar with it, that presence, that flow of power, of glory come down to attend the Word preached. As he lifted his voice, it filled his words like wind filling a sail, carrying them further and deeper than natural power could. He became energized, animated, carried aloft. All who were there felt it, for it penetrated their souls as well and made them hungry to never live apart from it.

Whitefield believed it had first come to him at his ordination. At the age of twenty-four, as he began to hit his stride in preaching, he reported after one particularly powerful meeting, "Now know I that I did receive the Holy Ghost at imposition of hands, for I feel it as much as Elisha did when Elijah dropped his mantle. Nay, others see it also, and my opposers, would they but speak, cannot but confess that God is with me of a truth."[12] For the next thirty-two years, it is what he speaks of most regarding his preaching. Time and again he recounts how the Spirit came in power, how his preaching was attended with the Divine presence, or how times of refreshing came from the presence of the Lord.

But he knew he was nothing without it. He often wrote of how he "spoke with little effect" or how his words "fell to the ground." It was as though God was testing him, leaving him to his own strength for a while to show him his total dependence. "Sometimes I perceive myself deserted for a little while, and much oppressed, especially before preaching," he wrote, "but comfort soon after flows in."[13] This refrain—"I was deserted before I went up into the pulpit"—is often repeated. Yet it seems always followed by, "but God strengthened me to speak." The lesson was never lost on Whitefield: "Lord, let Thy

Presence always follow me, or otherwise I shall be but as a sounding brass or a tinkling cymbal."[14]

Indeed, there was such a difference between White-field anointed and Whitefield unanointed that he would do anything to be where the grace to preach was upon him. We know that he started preaching in the open air because the clergymen refused him and the church buildings wouldn't hold the crowds. He quickly discovered another reason, though. He found that the Spirit of God was strong upon him in the fields. He sensed God's pleasure and felt it took the form of exceptional power. After one fruitful meeting he reported, "My own heart was much enlarged and the Divine presence was much amongst us; and indeed, I always find I have most power when I speak in the open air. A proof this is to me that God is pleased with this way of preaching."[15] The same was true when it came to speaking extemporaneously rather than from notes: "I find I gain great light and knowledge by preaching extempore, so that I fear I should quench the Spirit did I not go on to speak as He gives me utterance."[16]

We must recall that this man who often said, "I felt the Holy Ghost come upon me" or "the Spirit came with demonstration of power" was no overheated pentecostal or charismatic. He was an ordained priest in the Church of England. He was a man who preached the creed and the thirty-nine articles of his church. He was a man of liturgy and tradition and truth. Yet he had learned that truth and power must merge for lives to be changed. His life, then, becomes a challenge to all who would seek the one to the exclusion of the other.

ACTION

"There is not a thing on the face of the earth that I abhor so much as idleness or idle people." [17]

H E PREACHED more than eighteen thousand sermons in his lifetime. He rose at four in the morning, was often preaching by five, and seldom spent less than forty hours a week in the pulpit. In fact, the day of his son's funeral he preached three times and was preaching as the bells rang for the service itself. He traveled to America seven times, to Scotland more than a dozen times, and made other trips to Ireland, Bermuda, and Holland. Add to this the time spent on letters, journals, personal counseling sessions, building schools, training leaders, and just the business of getting from one place to another in the eighteenth century and it becomes clear that George Whitefield's life was a continuous explosion of divine energy.

Charles Spurgeon wrote, "He lived. Other men seem to be only half-alive; but Whitefield is all life, fire, wing, force."[18] It was true. George Whitefield was spiritual fire in motion, energy personified. It is hard to find an equally productive man in the pages of church history.

He may have first acquired this hard-working nature serving in the Bell Inn at Gloucester. To work for demanding family members while serving the needs of impatient guests must surely have schooled him well in the art of filling every minute with productive labor. This training was perfect preparation for the Methodists. The Methodist view of holiness taught that belonging to God meant serving him with time well spent. Each day was an altar and all the activities in it a sacrifice before him. Idleness was sin, entertainment an abomination. Time was the gift holy men offered to their God and Whitefield determined to worship Him well.

He couldn't understand people who lived otherwise. It is typical of him to write in his journal, "Oh, how swiftly has this week passed off! To me it has been but as one day. How do I pity those polite ones who complain that time hangs heavy upon their hands. Let them but love Christ, and spend their whole time in His service, and they will find no dull melancholy hours."[19]

The modern world might call this being driven, but it is instead the energy of a man who has glimpsed a God so great that he is worthy of all that man can give. For Whitefield, this meant not only time but excellence: "Whatsoever is done for God ought to be done speedily as well as with all our might."[20] It is the principle of a man who is not trying to save his life, not trying to infuse it with meaning for himself. For him, life is worship, like a sacrifice of sweet incense that is lifted to God by ever doing, ever acting, to his glory. Time ceases to be an enemy to conquer and becomes a holy offering on an altar of sacrifice.

"I find that action is the best way to take all oppression off the spirits," Whitefield wrote.[21] Throughout his *Journals* we find him recovering his sense of balance in activity. This is neither escape nor the self-deliverance of the workaholic. It is a man affirming that he is the creature, not the Creator. It is Whitefield declaring that there are burdens that are not his, cares he cannot bear, but that he knows his place of humble service to the One who bears all. When in doubt, when tossed and assaulted from every side, leave it to God and keep working.

George Whitefield lived only fifty-six years and ministered publicly for only thirty-four of those years. Yet during that time, he changed the course of nations, founded institutions that survive to this day, and dug wells of revival that refresh even now. All this was possible because Whitefield believed that to lose one's life for Jesus meant surrendering every moment of the time in which that life is measured. It is why he always said to those who urged him to slow down, "It is better to wear out rather than rust out."[22]

Spiritual Disciplines

*"Whosoever despiseth small acts of bodily discipline,
it is to be feared, will insensibly lose his
spiritual life by little and little."* [23]

THE SHIP hardly moved. The fresh food was gone. Each man was rationed a quart of water a day. People grumbled and complained and children screamed. It was miserable. And what did George Whitefield write in his journal? "I hope now the spiritual man will grow, having so little for the natural man to feed on." [24]

It was typical, both of him and the entire movement called "Methodist." It had all begun with the Holy Club, that band of seekers John Wesley led at Oxford. They met for prayer and accountability, true, but their most distinctive feature was their systematic approach to godliness. They sought a "holy Method of dying unto themselves and living unto God" and this meant sacrificial living and bodily discipline. It marked Whitefield all his life.

He hadn't started well. During his Oxford years, beset as he was with a false vision of spirituality, he had fasted himself nearly to death. In fact, his dietary extremes left him with stomach trouble for the rest of his life. He sought deliverance in excess. He slept in the cold, denied himself all comforts, and often "went nasty" or without regard for his appearance. He failed to turn in assignments thinking this a true sign of humility and kept his distance from friends thinking this true separation unto God. All such hardships failed him.

Yet, when he experienced the new birth, he began to understand the liberation to be had in the Spirit-empowered disciplines. He wanted more of the Jesus who dwelled within, but the flesh and its demands worked against him. His appetites seemed to drown out the drawing of the Spirit, and the needs of his body eclipsed the needs of his heart. To be the man he was called to be, he had to master himself, to tame his lesser drives so that his higher passions could shape his life.

It began with his use of time. He started "to live by rule more than ever, for nothing I find is to be done without it."[25] It meant organizing his time into a productive scheme and following it without deviation. It seemed to serve him well. When he pastored a church in his early years, he "divided the day into three parts—eight hours for study and retirement, eight hours for sleep and meals, and eight hours for reading prayers, catechizing, and visiting the parish. The profit I reaped by these exercises . . . was unspeakable."[26] The fruit of such living so impressed him that he lived by rule whenever he could. It did much to make him the productive, spiritually vibrant man he was.

He also knew the power of solitude. Though he was one of the most public men of his age, he knew that the true work of spirituality is done in secret, in the hidden places of prayer and contemplation. He made the time to deepen by rising early in the morning, by redeeming every spare moment for prayer and study, and by sacrificing sleep on the altar of piety. Nights of a few hours' slumber but many hours' prayer were not uncommon. He gained so much power through these hidden hours that he learned to sense when God was drawing him aside. He knew it was preparation: "I have observed that before God calls me to a public work, He always sends me into some retirement."[27] This, he knew, was the pacing of God, the metronome of the Holy Spirit for his life.

For Whitefield, a disciplined life also meant a life of moderation. This was difficult in an age of excess and for a man of Whitefield's fame. Though he often gave himself to seasons of fasting, he found that the fasted life—that lifestyle of consistent moderation—served best to protect his soul from the lures of the world about him. He lived simply. His clothes were always neat but never ostentatious. He often ate cow heel and laughed at how people would marvel if they knew that the famous Dr. Squintum, the man accused of living for lucre, was content with such a meal. He lived most of his thirty-four years of ministry in rented rooms or as the guest of strangers. His friends were often frustrated that he gave so much away. For Whitefield, this was simply how a man lived if he wanted to win the world. He believed that both the lost and his enemies would be won by "moderation and love and undissembled holiness of life."[28]

It should not surprise us that Whitefield's example is seldom followed today. It is costly. It requires a complete inversion of what we have come to expect of the visible and the great. It requires meeting riches with simplicity, fame with solitude, and luxury with moderation. It means viewing sacrifice as an investment in the invisible, an earthly planting in hopes of a heavenly reward. It is the way men live who long to live lives of eternal consequence in an all too temporary world. It is, more simply, the way of Whitefield.

UNITY

"The partition wall of bigotry and party-zeal is broken down, and ministers and teachers of different communions join with one heart and one mind to carry on the Kingdom of Jesus Christ. The Lord make all the Christian world thus minded! For till this is done, I fear we must despair of any great reformation in the Church of God." [29]

*T*HERE IS a prayer that dots the pages of George Whitefield's *Journals*. Though it sounds strange to modern ears, it was almost the daily cry of his heart: "God grant that I may always be of a catholic spirit." [30] By this, Whitefield was not referring to the Roman Catholic Church, of which he was suspect. Instead, he meant the word "catholic" in the old Latin sense of "universal," "all-embracing," or "of interest to all men." He was asking that God might break in him the very narrowness and bigotry he saw weakening the body of Christ all about him. It was his way of echoing the prayer of Jesus that God's people might be one.

He had not always been of such a mind. He was, after all, a loyal son of the Anglican Church. When asked to speak in a Presbyterian church in the early days of his ministry, he had refused. He viewed Roman Catholicism as a whoring after the inventions of men and he had deep reservations about groups like the Moravians and the Quakers. When he began to travel widely, though, he found that labels and organizational ties rarely revealed a man's heart, that true believers were spread throughout all Christian bodies. He saw the revivals that arose under his preaching touching people of every background and this inspired him to believe that a day of glorious Christian unity might be at hand.

Whitefield became a champion of the dream. His *Journals* reveal that he routinely met with and encouraged every kind of Christian believer. He learned to respect the various Christian traditions and regularly deferred to them when his conscience would allow. During his ministry in Georgia, "he did not demand that German, Swiss, or French inhabitants conform to Anglican rituals of baptism but instead incorporated their national traditions into the Anglican liturgy."[31] When he ministered the Lord's Supper in an Anglican Church, he was thrilled when believers of other denominations joined in. Some wanted to receive the bread and the wine sitting rather than kneeling, as Anglicans do. "I willingly complied," he wrote, "knowing that it was a thing quite indifferent."[32]

For Whitefield, the chief issue was salvation. "Some of Christ's flock are found in every denomination. My only aim is to bring men to Christ, to deliver you from your false confidences, to raise you from your dead formularies, to revive primitive Christianity! If I can obtain this end, you may go to what church, and worship God in what form you like best."[33]

Though Whitefield welcomed all believers, they unfortunately didn't welcome each other. Presbyterians suspected Quakers and Moravians suspected Lutherans and most every group of dissenters suspected Anglicans. Whitefield tried to love them all, but found building unity among them one of the most difficult tasks of his life. It saddened him. "How much comfort do those lose who converse with none but such as are of their own communion," he wrote.[34] He became frustrated with the narrowness and the labels and even the judgments about his own actions: "If I talk of the Spirit, I am a Quaker! If I say grace at breakfast, and behave seriously, I am a Presbyterian! Alas! What must I do to be accounted a member of the Church of England?"[35]

Still, he held high the banner of "One Lord, One Faith." He preached often that believers ought "not to let bigotry, or party-zeal be so much as mentioned among them; for I despair of seeing Christ's Kingdom come, till we are all thus minded."[36] Everywhere he went he warned, "What infinite mischief have needless divisions occasioned in the Christian world! *Divide et impera* ("divide and conquer") is the Devil's motto."[37] He even told divisive anti-Catholic dissenters that "if the

Pope himself would lend me his pulpit I would gladly proclaim the righteousness of Jesus Christ therein!"[38]

The unity of the church will never be perfect as long as sinners fill its pews. Still, it may from time to time take men like Whitefield to remind us that God's will was never a divided family. Whitefield knew and proclaimed to a deeply broken church what each generation of believers must live out afresh: Jesus seeks a bride, not a harem.

CRITICISM

*"Little do my enemies think what service they do me.
If they did, one would think, out of spite
they would desist from opposing me."*[39]

I T IS amongst the cruelest ironies. A man responds to the call of God because love compels him. He wants to please his Master, true, but he also wants to heal hurts and make a difference in the world. Yet the moment he declares himself, the moment he first reaches to tend the needs of mankind, the battering begins. He has not done enough or his theology isn't quite right or his gifts aren't equal to the task or somehow he doesn't measure up. Then begins the test of his life, for if the man allows the criticism to seep unfiltered into his heart, it will harden him, making him distant and sour. In this state, he will never fulfill his calling, never do the good he has set out to do. He has to rise above, has to declare war on the human tendency toward despairing bitterness, and learn the truth all wise leaders know: criticism is a tool for fashioning greatness.

George Whitefield was the most famous man of his day . . . and among the most hated. In a crude and spiteful age, the barrage against him was particularly venomous. He was accused of all the usual misdeeds with money, women, and fame. But there was so much more. The strange squinting of the eyes that childhood measles left him caused the hostile press to call him "Dr. Squintum." There was even a play by that name, written to expose him to a jeering public. If he gained weight, he was a glutton. If he bought property for an orphanage, he was selfishly building an estate for himself. It was open season on Whitefield and all England seemed to take aim.

Among Whitefield's critics were some of the most famous men of the day. William Hogarth, the renowned artist whose prints give us a window into the character of eighteenth-century England, mocked Whitefield in two engravings, one called "Saint Money-Trap."[40] Poet Alexander Pope compared Whitefield's "harmonic twang" to the braying of an ass, and playwright Samuel Foote parodied "Mr. Squintum" as a "blockhead dealing in Scriptures as a trade."[41] Even the eminent Samuel Johnson joined the fray. Refusing to "allow much merit to Whitefield's oratory," Johnson insisted that the evangelist's "popularity . . . was chiefly owing to the peculiarity of his manner." Johnson suggested that Whitefield "would be followed by crowds were he to wear a nightcap in the pulpit, or were he to preach from a tree."[42]

Then, of course, there was the uniquely "Christian" kind of attack. For some believers, a man cannot simply be wrong about a few things; he must be evil, possibly even controlled by a spirit. Certainly, he is part of a broader conspiracy of darkness, perhaps in league with the Antichrist. He then becomes an enemy to drive out rather than a brother to restore. So it was with Whitefield, who surely heard the words "You have a devil" as often as he heard the word "Hello."[43]

None of this surprised Whitefield: "I should doubt whether I was a true minister of Christ, was I not opposed."[44] Yet had he been a lesser man, he might have been crushed and embittered by the barrage against him. The pain might have driven him from ministry early, leaving him a broken, angry man. But Whitefield had acquired that condition of soul for which criticism becomes an ennobling force. He had learned that criticism is like pain in the human body, giving needed information for healthy change. One can receive it as a blow and angrily nurse the wound. Or, one can regard the words as an eagle does a gust of wind—as a force upon which to fly still higher.

Whitefield expressed this attitude beautifully when he responded to one critic by saying, "I thank you heartily. May God reward you for watching over my soul; and as to what my enemies say against me, I know worse things of myself than they can say concerning me!"[45] Because Whitefield peered courageously into any criticism he received and applied the wise correction he found there, his opponents only served to better him. So it was that he rose above both them and the embittered lesser man he might have been to grasp the greater character his calling required. As the poet William Cowper wrote of him:

> Assail'd by Scandal, and the tongues of strife,
> His only answer was—a blameless life.

SUFFERING

"Suffering times are a Christian's best improving times."[46]

EVERY AGE has its gospel of ease. It grows from the natural human desire to wrap eternal truth around temporal pleasure. It transforms every human whim into the will of God and offers comfort as the chief reward of righteousness. But it is a false gospel, one that leaves men both weak and vain. It makes every hardship an intruder and every difficulty an offense. It cushions men from the very means God uses to fashion them in His image and give them lives of weight and consequence.

Likewise, in every age there are those who challenge the gospel of ease. Insisting that hardship is a redemptive tool in the hands of a loving God, these stalwarts rage against a gospel that merely sanctifies the materialistic stupor of the times. They call for a people who embrace hardship as the price of change both in themselves and in a fallen world. Moreover, they challenge believers to allow what they endure to liberate them from their lower selves, to free them from the merely earthly in pursuit of the truly spiritual.

George Whitefield understood what suffering could accomplish in his life. He was no masochist, nor was he fixated on an angry Old Testament God to the exclusion of a more loving version. Instead, he believed that "sanctified afflictions are signs of special love."[47] He had learned that God uses sufferings to "break the will, wean us from the creature, prove the heart, and by them God teaches His children, as Gideon by thorns and briars taught the men of Succoth."[48] He welcomed "useful trials" that "inured me to contempt, lessened self-love, and taught me to die daily."[49]

In fact, Whitefield came to perceive a relationship between hardship and spiritual power. He believed that trials came before blessings in an almost cyclical manner. It is not uncommon to find him writing in his journal, "I was filled with such love, peace and joy, that I cannot express it. I believe this was partly owing to some opposition I met with yesterday."[50] Similarly, he writes of having "the most violent conflict within myself that I have had at all. Thus God always prepares me for His mercies."[51] It became a principle that shaped his life: "I always observe inward trials prepare me for, and are the certain forerunners of, fresh mercies."[52]

So glorious had the fruits of suffering been in Whitefield's life that he came to understand hardship as part of how God fashions a leader: "We must be made perfect by sufferings. If we do not meet them in our younger days, we shall certainly have them in the decline of life."[53] In fact, a leader could only offer true comfort at times of suffering if he had discovered that same comfort in his own times of distress: "I find it necessary more and more every day that ministers should be tempted in all things, that they may be able experimentally to succour those that are tempted."[54] Most importantly, though, sufferings cleared the heart for a fresh vision of God: "O may God put me into one furnace after another, that my soul may be transparent; that I may see God as he is."[55]

To an age of ease, Whitefield's high view of hardship sounds extreme. Yet, what he lived and taught was nothing more than what Scripture proclaims: that offenses will come to all, that the Godly will be persecuted, that trials attend the righteous. There is comfort in his example, for suffering will grace every life. For the unknowing, suffering will amount to little more than the painful experience itself. For others, though, suffering will be a doorway, an opportunity to become cleaner, freer, simpler, and more powerful than before. It is this vision that allowed Whitefield to write, "We must not always be upon the Mount in this life."[56]

Intercession

"Intercession is a glorious means to sweeten the heart."[57]

*I*T IS an axiom of human conduct: success breeds imitation. Men seek to copy what they esteem and replicate what they value. Yet, men also tend toward laziness and ease. It makes them yearn for a quick and painless path to the hard-won victories of others. They seek short steps to success rather than long lives of honor, procedures rather than principles. They become soulless shadows of the original.

This is what many have done in pursuing the success of Whitefield. Thinking they have located the source of his greatness in one part of his being alone, they copy his style while neglecting his substance. They take his preaching but neglect his devotion. They imitate his networking but ignore his holiness, strive for his generosity but discard his humility.

Most of all, they miss his trust in the power of prayer. It was one of the great truths of his life. Whitefield knew without doubt that God yearns to act in man's behalf and has committed himself to do so in response to believing prayer. He understood that Christians have the supreme privilege of praying God's Kingdom to earth, of overcoming the lost dominion of Adam by claiming the earthly lordship of Jesus. It transformed him. He saw what a praying man might do and he determined to do it fully.

He viewed intercessory prayer as the long-range artillery of the Kingdom of God and gave himself to unceasing bombardment. He often prayed throughout the night, interceded particularly before new directions in ministry, and usually found himself fighting spiritual battles before natural ones began. Intercession leaps from most every page of his *Journals*: "interceded for absent friends and all mankind,"[58] "a night of most comfortable intercession,"[59] "intercession for near two hours,"[60] "The Lord filled my heart and enabled me to wrestle with Him in prayer for New York."[61] He is clearly a man completely given to prayer, driven to it by the press of his great calling. It is the sustenance of his soul, the method of his ministry, and the means of true spiritual revival.

Yet, for Whitefield, intercession is more than a technique or even a discipline. It is how a Christian lives, how he breathes his communion with God and his purpose on earth. He once wrote, "When the spirit of prayer began to be lost, then forms of prayer were invented."[62] It is this "spirit of prayer" that possessed his life. To hear his sermons or read his writings is to eavesdrop on a life of constant communion with God.

Times of prayer were also times of God's presence. A typical note in his *Journals* reports, "When we came to public prayer, the Holy Ghost seemed to come into the congregation like a mighty rushing wind, carrying all before it."[63] It is a common experience. During one all-night prayer meeting, "The power of God came mightily upon us, insomuch that many cried out for exceeding joy, and many fell to the ground."[64] In these encounters, Whitefield found the power and the direction he needed. He also found refreshing for his weary soul: "I was somewhat cast down, but afterwards recovered freedom of soul, by retiring and pouring out my complaints and petitions before the Lord Jesus."[65]

This confidence in the power of prayer made him value the intercession of others, as well. When he faced the challenges of revival in England, he knew that "a more effectual door than ever will be opened" because "Jesus Christ is praying for me."[66] It encouraged him that "almost every day persons of all denominations come to me, telling how they intercede in my behalf."[67] He often bolstered himself for trials with the knowledge that "millions are praying for me."

One searches in vain for the ways of ease in Whitefield's life. There are no simple techniques, no three-step methods. He cannot be reduced to a pattern or a formula. However, if there is a core truth, a single reality that best explains the astonishing impact he had on his world, it is this: George Whitefield was a man of prayer. He was a man of tears and wrestling and hour upon hour in the dark watches of the night. These are his methods, his keys to success, and those who would change their world as he did must do likewise.

Predestination

"As for my own part, this doctrine is my daily support: I should utterly sink under a dread of my impending trials, was I not firmly persuaded that God has chosen me in Christ from before the foundation of the world, and that now being effectually called, he will suffer none to pluck me out of his almighty hand." [68]

S MEN see God, so they live their lives. Some see a God of anger and wrath. They live their lives accordingly. Others see a God of sweetness and light. This, too, will shape how they live.

In the matter of salvation, some see a God who has provided forgiveness in Jesus but who leaves men to discover it on their own. They must choose to be saved, exercising their free will to take hold of what is offered but not forced upon them. God is gentle, unobtrusive, suggesting what is best for man but never insisting.

Still others believe that man is far too fallen to ever choose what is right. Their God is an all-knowing, all-powerful God who would never leave the choice to men. Instead he chooses. He determines who will be saved. In fact, he has already chosen from before the beginning of time. This makes salvation a free gift, something a man cannot earn or work for, something he cannot take credit for finding. God chooses. God draws. God saves. God alone receives the glory.

This was the God of George Whitefield. Though he had come to faith in the heady mysticism of the Holy Club, his own studies led him to different conclusions: "God was pleased to enlighten my soul, and bring me into the knowledge of His free grace, and the necessity of being justified in His sight by *faith only*." Whitefield's travels in New England, among the sons and daughters of the American Puritans, only deepened his convictions. From there he wrote, "Whatever men's reasoning may suggest, if the children of God fairly examine their own experiences—if they do God justice, they must acknowledge that they did not choose God, but that God chose them. And if He chose them at all, it must be from eternity, and that too without anything foreseen in them."[69]

Whitefield felt himself standing with Paul and Augustine, Calvin and Luther. He saw how predestination magnified God and humbled man. It was biblical, it was consistent, and it was transforming. It rested faith on the work of God and not on man. It made evangelism a partnership with the living God who had already chosen men to be saved, already destined the very souls to whom Whitefield preached. This was the true gospel,

Whitefield believed, the one on which he would base his salvation and his ministry. "It is the good old doctrine of the Church of England. It is what the holy martyrs in Queen Mary's time sealed with their blood, and which I pray God, if need be, that I and my brethren may seal with ours."[70]

This faith in predestination spilled out into all of his life. He could say "We are immortal till our work is done" because he believed that a God who saved sinners also preserved saints. It made him courageous. It made him willing to preach anywhere under any conditions to anyone. Only God knew who was chosen. Whitefield's job was to preach knowing God would use the "foolishness of preaching" to reach appointed hearts. The results didn't depend on him. In fact, modern ministers are often surprised that Whitefield never asked people to respond in some way to his message, that he never gave an "altar call." He didn't need one. His job was neither to change hearts nor count those that were. His job was to preach the gospel. The rest he left with God.

It was a theology that cost him dearly. His friend, John Wesley, read the Scriptures differently and preached against election. It broke Whitefield's heart. The two leaders corresponded but could not reconcile. Followers chose up sides, the movement split, and the fires of revival dimmed. It was among the most painful experiences of Whitefield's life. Though he and Wesley were later reconciled, untold damage had been done and Whitefield learned the bitter lessons. "Let a man go to the grammar school of faith and repentance, before he goes to the university of election and predestination. A bare head-knowledge of sound words availeth nothing. I am quite tired of Christless talkers."[71]

George Whitefield was one of the greatest evangelists in church history. He also believed that God determined who would be saved before the world began. It seems contradictory. Even his friends said this view seemed to make evangelism unnecessary. Yet, in Whitefield's mind, the work of an evangelist and the doctrine of God's grace were one. Man preaches to hearts God has already prepared, already chosen. Salvation does not depend on the skill of a preacher or the will of man. It is God's work, a God who uses the foolishness of preaching to reach men so lost they could never choose for themselves. It was the mystery of salvation. It was the glory of God. And for Whitefield, it was the joy of his calling.

Courage

*"Every Christian ought to bring light and heat with him,
like the sun, whithersoever he comes. Wicked men
will show us an example of boldness."* [72]

H E WAS just passing by. His friends had already told him that if he preached again the people of Basingstoke would kill him. It was good that he kept moving. Still, the scene bothered him. Workers were building a stage for wrestling matches to be held later in the day and Whitefield just couldn't let it go. He rode on against the flow of people streaming to the bloody event, but he had no rest in his spirit. He prayed and finally could stand it no longer. "I could not bear to see so many dear souls for whom Christ died ready to perish and no minister . . . to interpose." He turned his horse about and hurried back to where the crowd was gathering. He had no choice: "I was resolved . . . to bear my testimony against such lying vanities, let the consequences as to my own person be what they would."[73]

He arrived at the site, mounted the stage, and began to plead for the souls of those gathered. Chaos ensued. A group of boys began to shout him down. A man leapt to the stage and beat him with a club. There was pushing and shoving and the angry shouting of a bloodthirsty crowd. Finally, Whitefield relented. "At last, finding the devil would not permit them to give me audience, I got off and after much thronging and pushing me, I mounted my horse, with the inward satisfaction that I had now begun to attack the devil in his strongest holds and had borne my testimony against the detestable diversions of this generation."[74]

This was Whitefield the bold, the courageous lion of God. From our modern vantage point we do not think of the Christian ministry as a profession demanding great physical courage. A preacher might need moral courage but seldom is he called upon to place himself in the path of bodily harm or death. This was far from the case in Whitefield's day, for as one biographer has written, "Whitefield's entire evangelistic life was an evidence of his physical courage."[75]

We must remember the times in which he lived. It was a violent, crass, brutal age; one in which the beating of a chained bear with a club was common street enter-tainment and hangings drew huge, cheering crowds. The upper classes were callused and removed while the lower classes formed an angry, sadistic mob driven by the whim of the moment. It was a dangerous time to be publicly preaching messages of conviction and repentance on the street corners of England.

We must remember, too, how hated and persecuted the Methodists and preachers of revival were. They weren't just taken to court or criticized in print as they might be today. They were beaten and humiliated. Men hired drummers to drown out their preachers and stormed their meetings in drunken packs. Women were stripped naked and occasionally raped. Children were maimed. Buildings were set on fire, men were bludgeoned to death, and ministers were sometimes tortured. One of Whitefield's dearest friends, William Seward, was killed while preaching in Wales when someone threw a large rock and hit him in the head. Such tragedy was commonplace.

Whitefield was far from immune. It was standard fare for him to preach under a torrent of eggs, tomatoes, rocks, excrement, and rotten fruit. Parts of dead animals were often hurled at him, with the bodies of dead dogs and cats as a favorite projectile. Whitefield was nearly clubbed to death twice, stoned once, whipped at least a half a dozen times, and beaten a half dozen more.[76] Amazingly, these assaults were often engineered by the clergy or local magistrates, who used raucous crowds to drive the troublesome preachers out of their jurisdiction.

"We are immortal till our work is done" Whitefield often said and it is the key to his courage.[77] Left to himself he was a timid, even cowardly man. But he had seen God, and in seeing had come to understand the loving-kindness, the gentle care of the One he served. His God could protect him, and even if not, his life was little to offer in the cause of the great King. And so he preached to the hostile crowds and endured the excruciating attacks. But because he was faithful and bold, he was able to rejoice before the end of his life that "religion, which had long been skulking in corners and was almost laughed out of the world, should now begin to appear abroad and openly show herself at noonday."[78] This is the crown that adorns God's courageous forerunners in every age.

THE DEVIL

*"In the strength of my Master, I will now enter
the lists and begin an offensive war with Satan
and all his host."*[79]

FOR GEORGE WHITEFIELD, it was personal. Others
of his time might have ceased believing in a
devil, in an evil being who went about tormenting
mankind. They may have spoken of Satan as a mere
symbol or idea. But not Whitefield. He had seen the face
of evil, had heard the taunting cackle. He had survived
the dark night of the demons and seen the works of
wickedness in a million twisted lives. For Whitefield, the
devil was exactly who Scripture said he was and to
become a Christian meant joining the war for his
destruction.

Though strange to modern minds, perhaps, Whitefield's view of Satan was just what the Bible and the
Reformation had taught him to believe. The devil was an

angelic being who had been cast out of heaven before time began. He ruled a demonic kingdom intent upon frustrating the gospel and destroying all humankind. Yet, so great is God that he not only defeated this kingdom of darkness with the cross of Jesus, but he also uses the devil to serve his purposes. The devil, then, is both raging destroyer and divine tool, God's vicious enemy and God's sheep dog.

For Whitefield, the battle with Satan was first fought in his own soul. He expected the tempting and the oppression that were the tools of the dark trade, yet he also understood how overcoming the evil one made him a better man. "Satan has been very quiet this week past," he wrote in his journal, "and God has poured much comfort into my soul, so that I must prepare for fresh trials. O my dear Redeemer, grant that I may put on the whole armor of God, that I may withstand all the fiery darts of the Devil."[80] For Whitefield, defying the devil was like an obstacle course he must master on the path of his Christian growth. He knew each trial, each attack, could fashion him into the man he was called to be—if he only held to his Master.

Winning private battles often led to public victory. An example is the demonic drive to extremes. Whitefield understood that "the wicked one makes use of men as machines, working them up to just what he pleases."[81] Since the devil "generally ploughed with God's heifer," since he tried to destroy the works of God by driving them out of God's boundaries, men had to strive for the balance of Godly wisdom. Whitefield found that when "the Holy Spirit put into my heart good thoughts or convictions, he (the devil) always drove them to extremes. For instance, having out of pride, put down in my diary what I gave away, Satan tempted me to lay my diary quite aside. When Castaniza (a Christian author) advised to talk but little, Satan said I must not talk at all. So that I, who used to be the most forward in exhorting my companions, have sat whole nights almost without speaking a word. But when matters came to an extreme, God always showed me my error, and by His Spirit, pointed out a way for me to escape."[82]

Through these struggles, Whitefield came to know the ways of his enemy, came to understand what the apostle Paul meant when he wrote, "We are not unaware of his schemes."[83] It gave him wisdom for liberating others and for leading the movement God was then using to change nations.

Satan's most effective attacks often came in the form of distorted beliefs about God. If he could fashion a man's belief about God, he could fashion the man. Whitefield sought to expose this tactic to the light of biblical truth, proclaiming "how the devil loves to represent God as all mercy, or all justice. When persons are awakened, he would, if possible, tempt them to despair; when dead in trespasses and sins he tempts them to presume. Lord, preserve us from making shipwreck against either of these rocks."[84]

Whitefield had also seen, time and again, how "Satan must try all ways to bring the work of God into contempt."[85] As he led the mighty revivals then flooding England, he found that extremes were usually the tool the enemy used to defame the work of God. Once he was asked to visit a young man who had been put in a mental institution because he was "Methodically mad." It turns out that the young man had fasted for extreme lengths of time, prayed in such a loud voice that he was heard "four storeys high," and sold all his clothes to give to the poor. People suspected insanity, but Whitefield knew that "this is nothing but what is common to persons at their first setting out in the spiritual life. Satan will, if possible, drive them to extremes. If such converts were left to God, or had some experienced person to consult with, they would soon come into the liberties of the Gospel." In time, the young man was released from both his exaggerated piety and from prison, but only because Whitefield had first faced the same demonic drive in himself.

It is not going too far to say that Whitefield viewed the entire of his ministry as an assault on Satan and his minions. A particularly successful season of preaching meant that many "inroads have been made into Satan's kingdom. Many sinners convicted, and many saints much comforted and established in their most holy faith."[86] Evangelistic crusades were viewed as invasions to reclaim territory from the kingdom of darkness. When he began preaching in the open air because churches refused to open their doors to him, Whitefield saw both the challenge and the resulting victory in terms of spiritual warfare: "I now preach to ten times more people than I should if I had been confined to the churches. Surely the Devil is blind, and so are his emissaries, or otherwise they would not thus confound themselves."[87]

George Whitefield preached at a time when the devil had fallen out of fashion and men knew nothing of spiritual warfare. At just such a moment, Whitefield roused the sleeping church and called it into battle. He drew stark battle lines and taught an awakening people of their foe and the tactics of that foe's defeat. Yet what Whitefield did for his age appears to be necessary afresh in every generation if history is any guide. May it be then, that those of this generation say of their time what Whitefield said of his: "Well may the devil and his servants rage horribly: their kingdom is in danger."[88]

THE WORD

"God has condescended to become an author, and yet people will not read his writings. There are very few that ever gave this Book of God, the grand charter of salvation, one fair reading through." [89]

*I*T IS five in the morning. Gloucester is dark and quiet, hours away from the bustle of an awakening seaport town. Down a sleeping side street there is a small bookstore owned by the Harris family. A light is on in the upstairs window, strange indeed on this chilly waterside morning. Strange, but expected, for the window looks out from the room of George Whitefield, the young man who met Jesus at Oxford but a few months ago.

But what is he doing? He sits in a chair with his *English Bible* on his lap. He is pouring over it, forming the words aloud and burning the meaning into his heart.

Beside him is his *Greek New Testament*. He consults it, checking every word of the passage before him, learning its sense and its mood. Back and forth he turns, until he captures the fullness he seeks. Then, he looks to *The Commentary of Matthew Henry*, that classic of exposition and truth. He reads. He looks away, reflecting. He reads again, compares, turns a page, and looks back. Finally, when all else is done, he prays "over every line and word" making every statement a request and melting the passage into his soul. He will start again tomorrow and the day after until every line of God's Word is savored and stored.

So it began. When Whitefield preached forty or fifty times a week without taking time to prepare, he thanked God for these mornings. When he could quote long passages of Scripture for his dramatic recreations, he breathed a grateful prayer. These early years of feeding, and the daily disciplines he cultivated in God's Word, made him the man of faith, doctrine, and wisdom men came to revere.

It was John Wesley who first taught him to roar after the word of God. His Holy Club wanted more than "quiet time" or "daily devotions." They wanted to be transformed. They wanted answers and truth and life. Wesley told his charges to read the Bible on their knees and hold every syllable before God in prayer. He taught them persistence, that "if we read once, twice, or thrice, and understand not, let us not cease so, but still continue reading, praying and asking of others."[90]

The next step was to obey. Whitefield often said, "nothing has done more harm to the Christian Church than thinking the examples recorded in Holy Scriptures were written only to be read and not imitated by us."[91] Whatever Jesus commanded, the Holy Club did. Their detractors called them "Bible moths" because of their devotion to Scripture, but they didn't care. They visited the sick, ministered in prisons, cared for the poor, and struggled manfully to forgive. They blessed those who cursed them, lived in community, and gave themselves to the Word, prayer, fasting, and the Lord's Supper. They searched the Scriptures to find a mandate for action and their obedience became the channel of refreshing for whole nations.

The pinnacle of this devotion to God's Word, though, was to let the Spirit speak through the Scripture-filled heart. Whitefield's *Journals* are full of statements like "the following verses in particular were set home to my heart" or "Many particular promises God has made me from His word . . . flowed in upon my heart."[92] Time and again he received direction as the Spirit pressed the words of the Bible upon his mind so as to give direction and comfort. During one difficult sea voyage, he reports, "This morning when I awoke, the faith of Abraham was greatly pressed upon me; and the example of Daniel and the Three children . . . is continually before my eyes."[93] By allowing the Scriptures to "indwell him richly," Whitefield had yielded his heart to the vocabulary of God and thus opened his life to the voice of his Father. Critics charged that this was extreme, that God spoke only in the context of written Scripture. Yet he had experienced these "quickenings" of the word so many times and so reliably that they could not be denied.

For George Whitefield the Scriptures were more than just literature; they were containers of Spirit and power. They had the power to melt the heart, cleanse the life, and enflame the spirit. He knew this because he had experienced it. It made him bold to preach the Scriptures and to pray, as he often did before he spoke, "Oh, that the Lord may beat them down with the hammer of His Word, till the heart of stone be entirely taken away! Amen, Lord Jesus."[94]

THE SEA

"I would not have lost this voyage for a thousand worlds; it has been sweet and profitable to my soul."[95]

O F THE fifty-six years that George Whitefield lived, more than two years—some seven hundred thirty-two days—were spent at sea. At a time when transatlantic crossings were still novel and extremely dangerous, never done for pleasure, Whitefield crossed no fewer than thirteen times. His longest crossing, in 1744, took eleven weeks; his quickest still required twenty-eight days.[96] It was an astonishing record for anyone of his time who was not a professional sailor. But it was seldom a trial for George Whitefield. He loved the sea.

Like all leaders, Whitefield often needed more than just rest. He needed experiences of renewal and inspiration. He needed new images to inform his thinking, living symbols to lift his vision and frame his purpose. He needed wells of refreshing, and he found them, surprisingly, as he sailed the vast, mysterious oceans of God.

Among Whitefield's favorite passages of Scripture was Psalm107:20.

> They that go down to the sea in ships,
> And do business in great waters,
> These see the works of the Lord,
> And His wonders in the deep.

Inspired by this verse, sailing became for Whitefield more than merely a means of travel. It became a voyage into revelation, a grand symbolic drama played out on the vast blue stage of the sea. He almost apologetically reports that while he might have been tending other duties, "I stood upon deck and admired the wonders of God in the deep."[97] In another place, he notes, "Had delightful sailing, and very thankful that God called me abroad to see and admire His wonders in the deep."[98] He seems at times transfixed. It is more than just a landlubber's fascination with the sea. It is as though his soul is tuned in to the "voice" that is speaking through the watery creation, as though the sea and its creatures are the medium of his exchanges with God.

And what lessons the sea had to teach him! When once his ship's captain caught a dolphin, Whitefield noticed how quickly the beautiful animal lost its color as it died. "Just so is man," Whitefield wrote, "he flourishes for a little while, but when once death cometh how quickly is his beauty gone. A Christian may learn a lesson of instruction from everything he meets with."[99]

The sea also spoke of the Sabbath: "All the day the sea was entirely becalmed and everything about us seemed hushed and quiet, as though it would remind us of that sacred rest the day was set apart to commemorate."[100] On one boisterous night, the sea spoke of obedience: "Oh, that I could learn from winds and storms to obey my master!"[101] Often, the sea symbolized the mystery of God's purpose. After one particularly agonizing night of soul-searching aboard ship, Whitefield proclaimed, "Lord, Thy judgments are like the great deep!"[102]

At a time when Whitefield was feeling betrayed by friends and deeply alone, he found the faithful friendship he longed for modeled by the creatures of the deep. As he watched a shark trail his ship, he noticed that the huge fish was "attended with five little fishes called the Pilot Fish, much like a mackerel, but larger. These, I am told, always keep the shark company and what is most surprising, though the shark is so ravenous a creature, yet let it be never so hungry, it never touches one of them. Nor are they less faithful to him for if at any time the shark is hooked, these little creatures will not forsake him, but cleave close to his fins, and are often taken up with him. Go to the Pilot Fish, thou that forsakest a friend in adversity, consider his ways and be abashed. This simple sight one would think sufficient to confute any atheist in the world."[103]

Had the sea held no fascination for Whitefield, he would have spent two years of his life in smelly, cramped, bone-jarring hellholes with no higher purpose than transportation served by the experience. But Scripture had given him eyes of faith to see what others might not, ears to "hear" the speech of the creation. He drank in the meaning and the truth he found enacted around him, and it made him a better man, a better Christian, and a better leader. Whitefield found, as all leaders must, the wells of refreshing for both his soul and his destiny.

TEACHABLE

"I have been too bitter in my zeal. Wild-fire has been mixed with it, and I find I frequently wrote and spoke in my own spirit when I thought I was writing and speaking by the assistance of the Spirit of God." [104]

*H*E WAS already a celebrity in his early twenties, the most famous man in England at the age of twenty-five. He was young, he was passionate, and he was aggressive. He was an evangelist who painted with broad strokes, a zealot who saw the world in terms of black and white, good and evil, friend or foe. And he made mistakes.

He once said of an author with whom he disagreed that the man "knew no more of Christ than did Mohammed." [105] The author happened to be the Archbishop of Canterbury. He had heard bad things about

Harvard University and, having never been there, publicly declared the school's "discipline at a low ebb" and stated that "bad books are become fashionable."[106]

It got worse. When his son was born, he was understandably proud and carried away with the moment. Most new fathers are. But Whitefield went further. He had already decided to name the child "John" because he believed him, like John the Baptist, filled with the Holy Spirit even from his mother's womb. When the child was born, Whitefield prophesied from his London pulpit that the boy "shall not be ashamed to confess the faith of Christ crucified, and manfully to fight under his banner against sin, the world, and the devil; and to continue Christ's faithful soldier and servant until his life's end."[107] He made other such boasts and predictions, but within months the boy was dead. Whitefield looked like a braggart or, worse, like a false prophet.

George Whitefield made mistakes. He exaggerated. He overestimated the size of his crowds. He underestimated the Christianity of his critics. He spoke of what he did not know and often enlarged what he did know. And none of these failings were played out in secret. His every statement, true or not, echoed in the press and in the jeering of his enemies.

Like most leaders, Whitefield did what he did because he believed he was right. He possessed that inner certainty that makes leadership possible. No one follows the indecisive; no one is inspired by the uncertain. True leadership requires a clear vision, a working inner compass, and the ability to sound a certain trumpet. All these demand confidence in what one believes, an engaging assurance that wins others for the cause.

The problem is that, unchecked, confidence can breed arrogance and conviction can vaunt itself into stubbornness. Whitefield saw this in himself and abhorred it. He saw that, despite his eagerness to do good, he had hurt people, hurt his cause, and, more terribly, sullied the name of his God. "I am a man of like passions with others," he wrote, and "may have sometimes mistaken nature for grace, imagination for revelation, and the fire of my own temper for the pure and sacred flame of holy zeal."[108]

In time, Whitefield learned to let his mistakes make him a better man. He became teachable. He resisted believing in his own perfection, embraced the lessons his failings had to teach, and made the amends true humility demands. In short, he yearned to be Christ's more than he yearned to be right.

It was a wiser, tempered Whitefield, then, who apologized to the faculty of Harvard University that he had spoken "too rashly of the colleges and ministers of New England" and who said he was determined to "own and publicly confess my public mistakes."[109] To friends, he admitted, "Alas, alas, in how many things I have judged and acted wrong. I have been too rash and hasty in giving characters, both of places and persons . . . I have hurt the cause I would defend and also stirred up needless opposition."[110] And in tenderly reflecting upon his prophecies about his dear son, he later hoped that the lessons he learned "May render his mistaken parent more cautious, more soberminded, more experienced in Satan's devices;

and consequently more useful in his future labours to the church of God."[111]

From George Whitefield's successes we can learn many things. From his moments of triumph we can drink inspiration for our own times. But there is little that he offers us more valuable than the noble fashion in which he confronted his own foolishness. It is here, from this crucible of the inner man, that Whitefield bequeaths perhaps his greatest legacy to those who would live lives of equal grace.

MONEY

"The bank of heaven is a sure bank. I have drawn thousands of bills upon it, and never had one sent back protested." [112]

H IS ENEMIES accused him of getting rich on the backs of the poor. The truth was he spent an amazingly small amount of money on himself. He owned almost nothing, ate cow heel when he had a choice, and spent most of his personal income on books. Indeed, an independent audit once showed that he took only thirty-five pounds from his massive offerings for personal expenses. That was at a time when the pastor of even a small church could count on a hundred pounds. [113] George Whitefield didn't need that much. He had food and clothing and that, he wrote, "is all a Christian should desire." [114]

Yet, when it came to reaching people with the gospel or tending the poor, George Whitefield spared no expense. He raised astonishing sums during his ministry and gave as freely as the needs of people required. In his day, the clergyman was but a step above a beggar, ever seeking a handout for the leaky roof or the widows' fund. People grew weary of them. Whitefield broke the mold. If he needed a printing press, he bought it. If there wasn't a building big enough for the crowds he drew, he built it. He understood what others of his age did not: You cannot change the world with the second-hand generosity of a miserly church. The generous will take the land.

Still, big vision required big faith. His training began early. Though poor in his student days, he soon learned to pray for his material needs: "Whenever I wanted any worldly assistance, [I] pleaded the Scripture promises for the things of this life, as well as that which is to come, in the Name of Jesus Christ."[115] Provision came, and White-field reasoned that what worked for his personal needs could work for the needs of many. In time, he learned to pray earnestly for the huge sums he needed to travel, build schools, publish, hire staff, and fill the hungry mouths of his age. Indeed, the funds came, the needs were met, and a generation witnessed the largesse of God.

Whitefield also reasoned that if he had not because he asked not of God, the same might also be true of men. He grew bold in making the needs of others known to the crowds who heard him. He was over-whelmed at the result. Poor coal miners gave all they had for Georgia orphans they would never meet. Simple farm folk pleaded with him to take their last shilling for the poor of the cities. Whitefield wept at their generos-ity and determined that if they could give, so could the rich. He cultivated friendships with the noble and the highborn and when he had the chance he made the plight of the poor known to them. Unprecedented gifts came to him, which he spent as needs required: on the school for American Negroes, the orphanage in Georgia, the church building in Scotland.

His skill in fund-raising became legendary. When Benjamin Franklin attended one of Whitefield's meetings, he had already decided not to give for the Georgia orphanage because he believed it would be better built in Philadelphia. Franklin knew of Whitefield's "power over the hearts and purses of his hearers" and set himself against influence. Still, "I had in my pocket a handful of copper money, three or four silver dollars, and five [coins] in gold. As he proceeded I began to soften, and concluded to give the coppers. Another stroke of his oratory made me ashamed of that, and determined me to give the silver; and he finished so admirably that I emptied my pocket wholly into the collector's dish, gold and all."[116] Franklin noted that an acquaintance of his, who left his money at home fearing Whitefield's power, repented and turned to a friend to borrow money for the offering. The second man, a Quaker, replied, "Friend . . . I would lend to thee freely; but not now, for thee seems to be out of thy right senses."[117]

Whitefield taught his generation that money is a tool and that generosity is the coin of the Kingdom. It was a radical message. It challenged the parsimonious ways of a beggarly clergy and called men to productive living to the glory of God. Soon men took the next logical step and understood that business itself is a calling, that profit of any kind is a trust granted by a generous Lord. It changed the ways of the church, and while there are always the charlatans and the greedy, what Whitefield taught has made possible some of the greatest endeavors in the history of the faith. Since his time, men have built great universities, purchased whole fleets to tend the needy, and funded missionary endeavors on an unprecedented scale. It is the legacy of a man who meant to show a starving world the richly provisioned table of his God.

BOOKS

"What are books without your Spirit, O Lord?"[118]

I T BAFFLED the crew. Every few days, that preacher fellow went to the side of the ship and threw something overboard. But what was it? How could a man living in such cramped space have so much to toss in the sea? It didn't make sense, but the man kept it up the whole voyage. And he seemed happy, almost giddy, as he committed his offerings to the deep.

Finally, someone had to ask and when he returned to the others laughing at what he'd discovered, the whole crew leaned in to hear. You see, that preacher was trading people their "bad books" for his good ones. He would offer his books on faith and holiness in exchange for a deck of cards or a sexy romance novel. No one took him up on it at first, but with every passing day the sermons and the exhortations and the casual conversations took hold. Soon, soldiers and debutantes alike found themselves giving up their carnal joys for the books in the preacher's bag. These were the trophies that crazy preacher, someone named Whitefield, threw to the fishes. Now the sailors understood, and soon they, too, went to their berths in search of something to trade.

Such stories were told wherever Whitefield went. Some joked that you could track the famous preacher by the books he left behind. In taverns and inns, on street corners and stages, he challenged people to cast aside their carnal pursuits and read the truths of God. Books were as much a part of his ministry as sermons and those who know his life understand why.

He fell in love with reading early. His best friend's father, a man by the name of Harris, owned a bookshop where little George marveled at the gold-embossed volumes standing row upon row like soldiers at the ready. What mysteries they contained, what adventures! He invaded their secrets, reading whatever he could. Fascinated with romances, he also read "plays, *Spectators*, Pope's *Homer*, and such-like trifling books."[119] He even bought books with money stolen from his mother's purse.

When he arrived at Oxford, he indulged himself in great literature and spent much of his meager earnings on books. It was books as well as spiritual hunger that connected him so tightly to Charles Wesley. After their first meeting, George left with a borrowed volume in hand and it wasn't the last treasure he took from Charles's shelves. Indeed, it was there he found Henry Scougal's *The Life of God in the Soul of Man*. How that book stirred him, angered him, accused him! We can see him reading it, putting it down, pacing around it and returning again. Ultimately, it captured him and imprinted one of the greatest of ironies upon the pages of church history: that the man who led thousands to faith by his spoken words was himself led to faith by a book.

From the earliest days of his Christian life, books discipled him. He loved the fellowship and encouragement of the Holy Club, but in the words of the great saints he found the truths that enflamed his soul. He basked in Thomas A'Kempis's *The Imitation of Christ*, drinking deep the rich wine of Christ's presence. He ransacked the treasures of Matthew Henry's *Commentaries* and found truer insight into Scripture than in the lectures of any Oxford don. Along with his Greek New Testament, these works were always with him. Friends wondered at the bag of books that made every ocean crossing, every horseback journey, and every country preaching tour. But these were his tutors, his friends, his needed soul support. They would go where he went.

And there were others. Indeed, Whitefield mentions so many books in his journals that one is tempted to forget how hectic his life was. He comments on Baxter's *Call to the Unconverted*, Castaniza's *Spiritual Combat*, and Francke's *Against the Fear of Man*. William Law's *Serious Call to a Devout Life*, *On Christian Perfection*, and *The Absolute Unlawfulness of the Stage Entertainment* receive particular attention. There is Alleine's *Alarm*, Janeway's *Life*, and Arndt's *True Christianity*. History features prominently in his lists with works like Archbishop Cranmer's *Life* and Foxe's *Book of Martyrs*. Indeed,

Whitefield recommended so many books that it seems impossible he read them all: Solomon Stoddard's *A Guide to Christ*, Jonathan Warn's *The Church of England-Man Turned Dissenter* and *Arminianism the Backdoor to Popery*, Jenks's *Submission to the Righteousness of Christ*, Hall's *Christ Mystical*, Eerskine's *Sermons,* and dozens more.

Yet, Whitefield did more than read and distribute. He published. He wrote forewords to his favorite books, made deals with publishers to keep important works in circulation, and even funded the printing of books he believed too important to leave to the market. At times he bought entire magazines and even whole printing presses to meet the literary demands his ministry created. His own journals and sermons were a publishing phenomenon, possibly the most widely distributed literature in England to that time. He used this reputation in publishing to urge "good books over bad" and to call publishers to serve Christ with their trade. And always, at every opportunity, he traded his books for those of the devil with every ploughboy, every scullery maid, and every tavern keep who was willing.

Whitefield's ministry merged the printed and the spoken word into a weapon of astonishing power. Centuries after his death, his journals, his printed sermons, his forwards to great books, and the hundreds of books he cajoled into print still serve to shape the Christian world. But it was more than just a love of the book itself that drove him. It was a love of truth and the words that carry that truth like an arrow into the hearts of men. One wonders what a twenty-first-century

George Whitefield might make of the tools of modern media. How would he have used the Internet or the other wonders of the digital age? We cannot know, but we can be sure he would use whatever means possible to fulfill his single purpose—to liberate captives with the artillery of God's Word.

Humility

"Lord, give me humility or I perish." [120]

I

T was a voyage in hell. First, there were the storms so violent they washed the provisions overboard and ruined the rigging. Then, the doldrums—no wind, no current, no movement. Frustration. Bickering. The small supplies of food and water dwindled. The cold came, biting and stinging. The starving passengers were gripped by a fear that grew into terror when the captain announced he had no idea where they were. Then the tearing of the sails and the taunting of the wind. Men searched their souls and prepared to die.

Finally, an anguished cry, half in anger, half in hope: "What Jonah have we here on board?"

It had come to this. The judgment of God. And who was the rebel who had drawn down the wrath of the Almighty?

"I am he," a voice rang out. And when all turned to see who had spoken, they saw George Whitefield, the most famous man in the world, the preacher who had called thousands to the saving grace of God.[121]

It was no act. Nor was he trying to draw to himself the ire better deserved by others. The reality is that George Whitefield truly saw himself as small in his own eyes and this is perhaps the best explanation for the astonishing spiritual power that distinguished his life.

His journals are filled with references to his "vileness" or his "actual sins and natural deformity."[122] He knows he is nothing apart from God. When he fails to sing a Psalm before a hostile crowd, he later writes, "Where was my courage then? Lord what am I when left to myself?"[123] Sometimes his sense of smallness in the face of a great task overwhelms him: "The thoughts of my own weakness, and the greatness of those trials which I must necessarily meet with, fill me with a holy fear. But wherefore do I fear? The Eternal Almighty I *am* hath and will no doubt protect me?"[124]

As humble as he was, he ever sought to be more humble. His constant prayer was, "Lord, keep me from climbing."[125] At times he cried out, "Lord, give me humility though it be through sufferings! So shall Thy blessings never prove my ruin."[126] He seemed almost eager to be humbled, as though he knew the glory on the other side was worth the often painful process: "This day I have been exalted, I must expect now to be humbled. Anything is welcome to me that God sends."[127]

Humility was such an important pathway for him that he spent much time reflecting on it. He knew it was first of all a humility before God. He had learned this the hard way, by resisting and paying the price. He once wrote with resignation, "I find all uneasiness arises from having a will of my own. And therefore I simply desire to will what God willeth. Oh! when will this once be."[128] Yet, he also understood that humility is lived out before men, as well: "I find more and more that true humility consists in being submissive to those who are a little above or a little below us. Oh, when shall I come to rejoice in others' gifts and graces as much as in my own!"[129]

This theology of humility, combined with a deep sense of his own weakness and folly, allowed Whitefield to do what less contrite men never could. Ever suspicious that his hearers might be "too fond of the instrument," he urged them to lift their eyes from the messenger to the God who made the message possible. And so they did, in numbers beyond any known in the history of the Christian faith. He sought no movements in his name nor monuments to his greatness because he knew that all such intentions made merchandise of the gospel. Understanding how quickly reverence in one generation becomes idolatry in the next, he often insisted, "Let the name of George Whitefield perish so long as Christ is exalted."[130]

The humility of George Whitefield was more than a studied style. It was the condition of heart that comes of seeing God and knowing oneself by comparison. This inner posture, this humility, not only freed Whitefield from the burden of self but allowed him to envision possibilities a greater pride never would.

Armed with such vision and the power that humility permits, Whitefield changed his world, and showed generations to come the path to true greatness in the Kingdom of God.

DIVINE DRAMA

"I speak as a dying man to dying men." [131]

LOOK AT the crowd that now awaits George Whitefield. They press about the table that will be his pulpit in the field that will be his church. There is a mixture of lifetime boredom with momentary curiosity in their faces. They are common and dirty and plain. They are the tillers of the fields or the milkmaids of the manor or the drovers of the herds. They sleep on straw, seldom bathe, eat the roughest food, and own little beyond what they wear.

And they cannot read. In fact, many will pass their entire lifetimes having never seen a printed page. The world beyond experience has come to them through stories, through tales they heard in childhood or legends relived over ale. They know their world through symbols and scenes from the stories of their time. In fact, for most of them, the best part of being in church is the chance to stare at the stained glass windows, brilliantly colored literature for an illiterate age.

It is the moment George Whitefield was born for. He mounts his pulpit in the field, throws back his robe, and lifts his voice like a trumpet. There are other great orators serving the church, but the crowd senses immediately that this one is different. Before they know what is happening, they are *seeing* his words. It is as though the mind is a stage and his words the actors who play there. The throng giggles with delight. Some shout warnings to the characters in Whitefield's stories, others weep for the fate of Job or wince at the crucifixion, images they have never before *seen* in such bright detail. When he is done, their hearts are melted and they are ready to live out the meaning of the pictures newly printed on their souls.

In a largely illiterate world, George Whitefield became his own text. One biographer called him "the divine dramatist." People of his time called him "the greatest actor of our age." He did not preach the gospel only; he recreated it. He stood before a crowd and showed them the drama of the truth, the theater of God reaching for man.

Even those who didn't understand his words still captured his meaning. One German woman who spoke no English reported to her pastor that from the great evangelist's "gestures, expressions, looks, and voice," she gained the "vivid impression that he was serious and sincere in what he said." She had never in her life felt "such a quickening, awakening, and edifying experience as when she listened to this man."[132]

Whitefield was a master at the power of story. He not only told tales from Scripture, modifying his voice to play every part or providing his own sound effects, but he also used the language of the audience before him to capture lost souls. Once, when he was speaking before a crowd of sailors, Whitefield used his knowledge of the sea to reach them: "Well boys, we have a clear sky, and are making fine headway over a smooth sea, before a light breeze, and we shall soon lose sight of land. But what means this sudden lowering of the heavens, and that dark cloud rising from beneath the western horizon? Hark! Don't you hear the distant thunder? Don't you see those flashes of lightening? There is a storm gathering! Every man to his duty! How the waves arise and dash against the ship! The air is dark! The tempest rages! Our masts are gone! The ship is on her beam-ends! Then what next?" The sailors rose from their seats as though scrambling from the crashing waves and shouted, "Take to the life boat, Sir. Take to the life boat."[133]

Even the literate upper classes were drawn in. When Whitefield was once preaching to a gathering of nobles in the home of Lady Huntingdon, he made the point that a man without Christ resembled a blind beggar with a stick, using a little dog as a guide. The two walked on a grassy slope. The leash broke and the dog wandered off. The blind man had to feel his way. He drew near a cliff and accidentally dropped his stick. Hearing no echo because the drop-off was too deep and thinking the stick had fallen in soft mud, the blind man leaned over to pick it up. He lost his balance, his foot slipped . . . "He's gone!" a pained voice yelled. The startled gathering turned to see whose panicked voice had interrupted the preacher. It was none other than Lord Chesterfield who, like millions of lesser repute, found himself swept into Whitefield's play.

This story became famous in England, as did hundreds of vignettes and skits played out in the pulpits of the land. Whitefield's method became so well known that crowds came to anticipate the word that pulled back the curtain on his theater of the heart: "methinks." When Whitefield spoke this word, he left the literal sense, left the exposition and the fact, and moved to the recreations that set his meaning ablaze. With the phrase, "Methinks I see . . . " Whitefield would envision Abraham in heaven or the return of the prodigal son. The bloodied body of Jesus might lie right before his listeners, with Whitefield's words pressing the tragedy home to every heart.

Nor were words all that Whitefield used. Unlike the staid clergy of his day, he stirred with every dramatic turn, whipping his black robe about, thrusting his arms, drawing action in the air. For props he used what lay about him: a horse standing near the stage, a boy sitting at his feet, even the helmet of a transfixed soldier. As pure entertainment it was the best the common man would ever see. As medium of the divine message, it touched hearts as the "polite preachers" of the age never had.

George Whitefield knew that while the Christian message never changes, the Christian method must. Every generation must refashion its medium to fit eternal truth to temporal setting. To do otherwise is to make an idol of the past and to miss the glorious opportunities of the present. Had Whitefield preached in the manner of his time, millions might have ended Christless lives in a hellish eternity. Yet, because Whitefield understood his moment, understood that stories could do what traditional sermons could not, he reached the masses of his age and rescued a race descending into darkness. For Whitefield, though, his task was simply to preach with all the passion, drama, movement, and desperation of a "dying man to dying men."

Feeling Truth

"Had I in mind to hinder the progress of the Gospel and to establish the kingdom of darkness, I would go about telling people they might have the Spirit of God and yet not feel it." [134]

ENTHUSIASM. IT was the dread enemy of the church. The word meant everything from "unrestrained passion" to insanity and every priest, bishop, and sexton feared it as much if not more than the devil. In an age when Christianity was little more than fine manners, worship little more than remembrance of things past, enthusiasm was the great enemy of that quaint sentiment some called faith.

Then came George Whitefield. His search for Jesus had cost him too much to ever settle for mental assent. At Oxford he had nearly fasted himself to death. In what he thought was humility he had done good works and slept in the cold and tended the poor. Good had come of it for others but he was left empty. Then he read Henry Scougal's *The Life of God in the Soul of Man.* It made him furious. Scougal suggested that Whitefield's religion was one of the outward man only, that he had missed the point of the gospel. How dare he! But Whitefield read on: "True religion is a union of the soul with God, a real participation of the divine nature, the very image of God drawn upon the soul, or in the Apostle's phrase, it is *Christ formed within us.*"[135] Whitefield argued it, wrestled it, tried to dispense with it. Then, finally, surrender. And joy . . . joy unspeakable as Jesus "possessed my soul."

From that moment on, George Whitefield was a man on a mission. He had to rescue Christianity from the "manners brigade," had to cleanse it of all that hindered a living experience of Christ in the soul of man. People had to know that God longed to inhabit their souls, to fill the hungering heart with transforming love. All else was dead works or "historical faith," the sentimental recollection of events long past. But it wasn't Christianity.

For this Whitefield largely blamed the clergy. "I am persuaded the generality of preachers talk of an unknown and unfelt Christ. The reason why congregations have been so dead is because they have dead men preaching to them . . . How can dead men beget living children?"[136] His travels throughout the British Isles and to America confirmed this: awakened ministers gave birth to awakened congregations, men with the fire of God in their souls had fire to impart to their people. His travels "convinced me more and more that we can preach the Gospel of Christ no further than we have experienced the power of it in our own hearts."[137]

But what of the masses, of the millions who were enmeshed in the lifeless web of dead faith? Conventional wisdom said that they were too preoccupied with the business of life, that they would never tolerate, much less respond to, a "costly gospel." Whitefield knew better. He knew that every soul longs for filling, that every heart is restless until it finds its rest in God. So rather than preach sweet and comfortable sayings like other clergymen, Whitefield raised the bar, refusing to accept the mere affirmation of truth as the sum of salvation. "Every one that has but the least concern for the salvation of his precious, his immortal soul . . . should never cease watching, praying, and striving till he find a real inward, saving change wrought in his heart, and thereby knows of a truth that he dwells in Christ and Christ in him."[138] And men flocked to Whitefield's message, for the age of manners had merely masked an age of spiritual hunger.

To a church that feared passion above all, Whitefield preached the soul possessed by God. To a people left empty by polite sermons and lifeless ceremonies, Whitefield preached the inner feeling of divine love. And to an age that allowed the fire of the Reformation to nearly smother in the ash of respectability, Whitefield preached the transforming truth of the indwelling Christ. Let them call it enthusiasm. Let them ridicule. To Whitefield it was simply the gospel of Jesus and with it he set his world aflame.

THE POOR

*"I hope to grow rich in heaven by taking care
of orphans on earth."* [139]

*I*MAGINE. IT is 1745 and you are walking the
streets of London. You make a wrong turn.
Down a back street and through an alley, you find yourself . . .

> . . . *in a squalid confusion of buildings, fever-laden
> haunts of vice and wretchedness . . . a maze of
> alleys and lanes fading into the unwholesome vapor
> that always overhung them, of dirty, tumble-down
> houses, with windows patched with rags and
> blacked paper, and airless courts crowded with
> quarreling women and half-naked children, wallow-
> ing in pools and kennels.* [140]

The scene embosses itself on your mind. The squalor, the hunger, the human agony haunt you. The faces seem to crowd about you, piercing you with the hollow darkness of their eyes. It is more than you can stand. You walk on and find yourself on a main street. A bejeweled carriage goes by. You think on the grand manors of the rich. The callousness stabs at the heart. How can it be? How can such opulence exist beside such grinding horror? Can anything be done to change such a wretched wrong?

This was the world of George Whitefield. Wealth was a divine right, poverty a sign of divine disfavor. As the poor grew more numerous the rich grew more calloused and the nation reeled from the tension. To escape the vileness, men drank and drank hard. It was the day of the "Gin Craze." Every sixth house was a "gin house" and prints from the time show mothers even pouring the poison down the throats of their crying young. And the evil spiral continued: the prisons bulged, the poorhouses swarmed, the street urchins multiplied, and the idleness spread.

Then came the Methodists. They sought only to do what Jesus had commanded. He said visit me in prison, feed me when I'm hungry, clothe me when I'm bare. So, out they went to the darkness and stench. At first it was a shock. Officials at Oxford commanded them not to go. But Jesus said otherwise, so they went. In time, they pricked the conscience of the nation, but not before they cared for the prisoners of Britain almost single-handedly year after year.

Whitefield led the way. He knelt in prison cells teaming with rats and prayed broken men to Jesus. He read aloud as robbers wept and fed husbands and fathers

ars."[146] Still, he remained faithful and when a friend
[ask]ed how he survived, he sighed, "My father always
[said], when you make a bad bargain, hug it the tighter."[147]

Then there was the marriage of Whitefield's friend,
[Joh]n Wesley. It is not saying too much to assert that
[Wes]ley's wife was his worst enemy. An associate stopped
[at t]he Wesley home one day to take John to a meeting
[and] found his wife dragging the preacher around the bed-
[roo]m by the hair. Indeed, the woman often traveled to
[her] husband's meetings just to heckle him as he
[preac]hed. More than one historian has maintained that
[Wesl]ey's extensive travels were prompted in part by a
[despe]rate need to avoid going home.

[G]eorge Whitefield's marriage was neither the
[enti]cing nor the disrupting kind, but it was strange and
[it w]as largely Whitefield's fault. He had written a friend
[in 174]0, "I believe it is God's will that I should marry."
[He] added: "I pray God that I may not have a wife till
[I li]ve as though I had none." Here we see the tension
[that do]omed him, that made the whole of his love life a
[sad and] disappointing affair. He wants companionship
[but] distrusts himself. His Methodist training makes
[him fear] anything that could become an idol or that could
[steal] affections from his God. So, he hopes both to be
[married] and to live as though he were not. It is a sad
[and d]raining tension that is as much unnecessary as it
[is unbibl]ical. Unfortunately it robbed Whitefield of what
[might ha]ve been a glorious addition to his life.

[At] times he is painful to watch. He wrote the par-
[ents of th]e woman he hoped to marry that, "I am free

whose only crime was seeking the family food amongst
the refuse of the rich. He cheered General Oglethorpe
when he dreamed of an American colony for England's
debtors and built an orphanage when those debtors
abandoned their young. He preached in slave quarters,
squatted in Indian hamlets, and slept in the hovel of the
meanest highland farmer.

Perhaps as importantly, he stormed the bastion of the
rich. "Oh, the polite world," he raged. "How are they
led away by lying vanities."[141] He lifted his golden voice
and rebuked the wealthy hardened heart: "They had
rather spend their estates on their hawks and hounds, on
their whores, and earthly sensual, devilish pleasures,
than comfort, nourish, or relieve one of their distressed
fellow-creatures." He also showed them by example.
Believing that "the parsonage-house ought to be the
poor's storehouse," he lived an amazingly generous life,
once even giving away his family's furniture when
another had a need.[142] And he didn't stop with example.
He thought nothing of directly approaching the wealthy
in order to help the needy, it being "my constant practice
to improve my acquaintance with the rich for the benefit
of the poor."[143]

It is easy to see Whitefield and his Methodists as a
dizzy band of do-gooders who made no lasting difference.
But this is far from the case. Most historians agree that
England in Whitefield's time was growing increasingly
unstable, that the masses—often called "Sir Mob"
because of their raging power—were growing increasingly angry. It was a dangerous time. Many students of
the era agree that England was on the path of the French,

with a bloody revolution in its future. Soon came the guillotine and the hatred and the fear. But England was spared. She was spared because the gospel of Jesus, a truth that changed men's hearts and set them to their neighbor's burden, ranged free throughout the land. So rather than a revolution, England saw a golden age and soon could boast an empire the sun never ceased to grace.

Thus the revival that saved a nation. Even the critics admitted it, for as Whitefield's critic, Sir James Stephens, ultimately conceded of him, "If ever philanthropy burned in the human heart with a pure and intense flame, embracing the whole family of man in the spirit of universal charity, it was in the heart of George Whitefield. He loved the world that hated him, he had no preferences but in favor of the ignorant, the miserable, and the poor."[144]

MARRIAGE

"Marry when or whom you
expect trouble in the flesh

*T*HERE IS no question that a
a great man greater. Inde
measure what Clementine did for
did for Madison. How the wife of ;
insulate, and cultivate has often le
her husband but also on the cours

Yet the opposite is not equal
and a painful marriage do not n
men, for the fact is that some c
history have had gut-wrenchir
Abraham Lincoln. He was marri
made his life hell. When a trade
him of Mary's tirades, he replie
stand, for fifteen minutes, wl

from that foolish passion which the world calls love. I write only because I believe it is the will of God that I should alter my state." He then wrote the woman herself that "the passionate expressions which carnal courtiers use, I think, ought to be avoided by those that would marry in the Lord." This after listing all the pleasures the woman would have to give up if she married him. One historian has said, "Had he tried to design his proposal in such a way as to ensure its failure, he could hardly have done better."[148] Another has said that Whitefield was "as odd a wooer as ever wooed."[149]

When he ultimately married, he chose a woman whom he hardly knew and who was, in fact, in love with another man. They had probably spent less than a week together before marrying. He had sworn he "would not preach one sermon less in a married than in a single state," so during the week-long honeymoon he preached twice a day.[150]

Within two months of the wedding he wrote, "O for that blessed time when we shall neither marry nor be given in marriage, but be as the angels of God."[151] Before long his absences increased. She remained in London while he traveled. Once he was gone for two years. It was, as they both understood, a ministry marriage and the work always came first.

Still, there were the moments when something seemed to spark between them. When a mob stormed a meeting where Whitefield was preaching, he felt his courage begin to fail. Aware of a tug on his gown, he looked down to see Elizabeth, his wife. "George," she called, "Play the man for God."[152] It is a telling moment. It seems that she understood her husband's struggle and knew she could inspire him. How often she was able to is not possible to know, though she once admitted, "I have been nothing but a load and a burden to him."[153]

A man who lived with the Whitefields for some years reported, "He did not intentionally make his wife unhappy. He always preserved great decency and decorum in his conduct towards her."[154] It is a tragic epitaph, and those who seek to honor Whitefield do him no disservice by acknowledging it. George Whitefield was a great man, but his views of marriage were wrongheaded, even denying the intent of the One who made marriage for the good of mankind. How might he have lived had he embraced marriage as a source of grace? How might his life have been lengthened by the rest and joy of more time at home? What might have come from children born to a stable and loving home? We cannot answer these questions, but we honor Whitefield by knowing that they should be asked in our time as they might have been asked with great profit in his.

JESUS

"One thing is needful." [155]

I T GRIEVED his soul. The wealth and the worldliness, the disinterest and the pride, gnarled his inner being. He was fifty-one and had seen many things, but the rich family that hosted him in the little town of Southold typified all his fears. They were a materialistic people who had forgotten God. To own and enjoy was their greatest delight and it made them selfish and small. He wept for them, remembering the lesson Jonah learned, that "all who cling to worthless idols forfeit the grace that could be theirs."[156]

He slept fitfully throughout his last night in the grand house. When he arose the next morning, he decided he had to sound a warning. This family, like so many in the land, was losing its soul—one possession, one drink, one grasp at a time. Then it came to him, a message brief but enduring. He used a piece of diamond jewelry to write on a windowpane, "One thing is needful," quoting the words of Jesus to a distracted disciple. Though we cannot know the family's response to these words, we do know that they last until this day, that pane of glass surviving the centuries and giving testimony to the singular love of George Whitefield.

There are many emphases within the Christian life. Some love the cause of the faith and give themselves to the titanic struggles with paganism their age demands. Others love the community of faith and the human connections that faith binds in strength. Still others fix their gaze on eternity and celebrate the assurance of heaven all their days on earth. Each of these, and more besides, are paths within the Christian landscape. They are rooms men choose to occupy within the broader mansion of Christianity.

Yet, few, indeed, very few, chose as Whitefield did. He tried to embrace all that Christianity meant, but his one true love was always the person of Jesus. The risen Christ was the fixed star of his life's voyage, the sole object of his affections. It was Jesus for whom he lived, Jesus whom he sought to please, and Jesus in whom he hoped to find his rest. This distinguished him in an age of what John Wesley called "the half Christian," in a time of Christianity lived in bits and pieces rather than the whole that Jesus is.

It had always impressed Whitefield that a man who was also God sat at the right hand of the Father. Jesus was both the human who had ascended on high and the God who had made himself low. For both his divinity and his humanity, Whitefield loved him. He had read in the Old Testament of the Father's eagerness for all men to know his Son. This seemed the greatest of divine passions and Whitefield believed that the truest response of the faithful should be in reflecting that passion for intimacy back to the Son. This was the divine romance, the intimate dance that love for God created. "Draw me after you," Whitefield prayed to his Lord, "and let us run together."

This divine romance had practical meaning, also. So fastened to the glory of Christ was Whitefield's ethical sense that he easily bypassed temptations that entangled lesser men. In the days of the great revival, when factions arose, Wesley opposed, and his followers urged him to start his own movement, Whitefield would have none of it. He ended up giving his ministry property to Wesley, the very man who criticized him publicly, and refused to put his name on any organization.

Why? Why not lend your name to something worthy that would make your reputation survive rather than leave to a rival the honor of generations? For Whitefield, the answer was simple: the glory of Christ. He responded firmly: "Let the name of George Whitefield perish so long as Christ is exalted."[157] This was no mere slogan intended to impress supporters. It was the heartfelt desire of a man who had peered into the face of Jesus and knew the worth of glory. It was the horror of one who might touch that glory with the unclean hands of pride.

This love for Jesus also made him bold. He understood that nothing a man can suffer is worth what Jesus endured. He longed to make up what was lacking in the suffering of Christ, to live the courageous life of one who serves the Lion of Judah. "When the heart is full of God," he insisted, "outward things affect it little."[158] He loved being "on the stretch for God," thinking it an act of worship, feeling that somehow he honored in extremity better than at other times. This accounts for his joy in trials, his peace in turmoil, his extravagance in sacrifice.

It is a common mistake among those who study the great to imitate the method rather than the heart. In ministry, this is disastrous. A man might rightly duplicate the method of a famous engineer or businessman, because their fields are primarily about methods. But a minister is primarily about bringing others into a relationship. To imitate the method of ministry without absorbing the love for Jesus that ministry is means fruitlessness and a cancerous form of idolatry. Indeed, as Whitefield understood, passion for Jesus is the personal renewal from which greater revivals spring. Here, then, is the enduring lesson: relationship is the method.

EXCESSES

"Wild fire will necessarily blend itself with the pure fire that comes from God's altar." [159]

IT STARTED with his first sermon, a well-studied exhortation on the importance of Christian community. There was no reason it should be remarkable as first sermons go. True, he did experience "a heartfelt sense of the Divine presence" and he had long prayed for that crucial day.[160] But nothing could explain why after the short teaching fifteen people should claim to have been driven mad by the power of what they heard. It was mystifying, though the bishop hardly seemed to care. He simply quipped, "I hope their madness lasts until next Sunday."[161]

It did. In fact, whenever George Whitefield preached, people were affected in unusual ways. They would weep or groan with agony of soul. Some shook violently. Others fainted. Some seemed to pass out under the weight of conviction and then lay upon the ground as though dead for hours. Many screamed in horror thinking they were on fire or that the ground was opening up beneath them to plunge into the blazes of hell.

Whitefield saw these "agitations" as merely the soul's response to the convicting work of God. They were normal, he believed, when the Word was at work, when the Spirit of God was present, and when sinners were receiving their deliverance. You didn't encourage them. You didn't draw attention to them. But you did accept them as the by-product of revival, as the completely biblical response of an unclean people to a Holy God.

Then it grew worse. The unlearned and unstable, mistaking the outward sign for the inward reality, began to re-enact the strange actions of others thinking this was the path to power. The meetings grew increasingly boisterous. In time, crowds gathered to watch the affected who had become a show in themselves.

Wise leadership might have regained the high ground at this point, but it wasn't to be. Ministers began to see the manifestations as evidence of the Spirit's power, as confirmation of their own anointing and gifts. The race to the extreme had begun.

And no one was more extreme than the Rev. John Davenport. Though possibly unhinged by serious bouts of fever, Davenport made much of special revelations from God, of his knowledge of the "last days," and of his own particularly favored position with the Almighty. He chastised faithful pastors for their lack of conversion and sought to close their churches. Then the burnings began. Davenport insisted that every offending object in every offending home be burned. Huge bonfires were built to consume the evils of jewelry, books, wigs, clothing, and even, during one especially feverish spree, Davenport's britches!

Whitefield saw the destruction of God's work in these excesses and he opposed them. "The devil always plows with God's heifer," he said, meaning that evil often highjacks the good to do its work. Whitefield understood that though there is a fine line between spiritual manifestations and mere emotionalism, it must be observed, lest the work of God be both deformed and defamed.

This view brought him into conflict with his friend, John Wesley, who had come to see the intensity of the manifestations during his sermons as evidence of spiritual power. Whitefield urged him to reconsider. "I cannot think it right in you, Honored Sir, to give so much encouragement to those convulsions which people have been thrown into under your ministry," Whitefield insisted. Such preaching, he urged, would "take people from the written word and make them depend on visions, convulsions, etc. more than on the promises and precepts of the Gospel."

In time, Whitefield prevailed. Davenport repented, Wesley held a firmer line, and the revived put less stock in the by-products of revival than they did in the pure work of the Reviver. Still, an important lesson had been learned. Every movement possesses the power to destroy itself through its own excesses. Wise leadership must encourage the power, the passion, the pursuit of possibilities but guard against the extreme and the exotic for their own sake. Without boundaries, great outpourings simply become destructive floods. We want rivers, both spiritual and natural. But we also need riverbanks.

Hardship

*"I am never better than when I am
on the full stretch for God."* [162]

George Whitefield wanted above all to glorify his God. He knew this meant hardship and suffering. He could never have known how much.

It began when his father died. George was less than a year old. Then, seven years with no father at all followed by six years of hell under the abusive hand of his mother's new husband. Finally, divorce and shame to last a lifetime.

Then Oxford and the foolish extremes that damaged him for life. His fasting was so excessive that doctors had to confine him to bed for seven weeks. He prayed in the snow, denied himself sleep, and refused to tend his most basic bodily needs. His health was never the same.

His preaching career is one of the most torturous on record. It lasted thirty-four years. There was barely a sermon during which he was not opposed and opposed violently. Rotten fruit, dead animals, and manure filled the air when he spoke. He was beaten and left for dead. His wife was assaulted, his friends were killed, and his offerings were stolen.

If his *Journals* are any indication, he was almost always sick. He once wrote, "My body is weak and crazy."[163] After he preached he usually had "a vast discharge from the stomach, usually with a considerable quantity of blood."[164] He would often have to be carried to bed by friends who feared he would not see the next sunrise. The truth is he started most of his services in ill health.

He offered marriage to one woman only to find she had fallen in love with another man. When he finally did marry still another woman, he rarely saw her. During one season when she tried to travel with him the schedule was so grueling that she miscarried four times in sixteen months. Their only child died early and his mother died two years before her husband. It was by many accounts an unhappy union.

His best friends betrayed him. His mentor and friend, John Wesley, publicly questioned whether he was saved. The animosity permanently damaged his life's work. And it was personal. People he had led to Jesus passed him on the street in silence. This, combined with the plays, newspapers and clergymen who arrayed against him, made him the most hated man in England.

He suffered horrible accidents throughout his life. In Northampton, Massachusetts, his horse stumbled on a broken bridge and pitched him onto his nose. He lay stunned and bleeding as alarmed townspeople rushed to his aid. On a September day in 1743, Whitefield took his pregnant wife for a ride in a borrowed carriage. His mind almost certainly far away, he failed to notice a turn in the road and drove straight into a wide-open drain that descended steeply for fourteen feet. The carriage landed heavily. The panicked neighing of horses brought passersby, some of whom shouted, "They are killed!" It was not far from true, nor was it the only time that such accidents beset the Whitefields.

Moved with compassion for Georgia's orphans, he started an orphanage to tend their needs. It was a noble effort but it saddled him with burdensome debt for most of his life. Problems were unceasing. Trustees withdrew, supplies were stolen, and before he knew it Whitefield owed more than five hundred pounds— some twenty years' wages. At a moment of despair he declared, "I am almost tempted to wish I had never undertaken the Orphan House."[165]

Tragically, he grew old before his time. When John Wesley saw him on October 28, 1764, he noted that "Mr. Whitefield seemed an old, old man, being fairly worn out in his Master's service."[166] But Whitefield was only fifty. He suffered from asthma and angina and some undiagnosed condition that gave him a florid, rather puffy face. He grew heavy because of disease, but enemies said he grew fat on good living. His conditions made him irritable. He would recover himself, burst into tears and say, "I shall live to be a poor peevish old man and everybody will be tired of me."[167]

It is easy to recall the life of Whitefield and forget the hardships. The pain and the loss can understandably be missed among the glowing victories. Yet, to do so would mean failing to learn one of the most important lessons his life has to teach: that suffering is a source of power. As he often said throughout his life, "I never feel the power of religion more than when under outward or inward trials."[168] It is a challenge to those who would fulfill his legacy, a needed reminder in an age of the easy path.

GREATHEART

"The best of men are permitted to err, that we may know they are but men."[169]

I T WAS a typically Scottish arrangement. Two ministers shared the same pulpit of an Aberdeen church, one a Whitefield supporter, the other a Whitefield hater. It so happened that the Sunday Whitefield was in town, the minister who supported him was in charge of the morning service and the famous evangelist was given the pulpit. But the other minister, Rev. Bisset, had the afternoon service and Whitefield, sensing he was in for a scorching, attended the service of his enemy as was his custom.

It was in the middle of the opening prayer that the barrage began. The congregation heard Bisset ask God's forgiveness that George Whitefield had ever been allowed to preach, for the blasphemy of such a scoundrel speaking in such a holy place. Then the sermon began and Bisset tore into Whitefield like a vicious animal, reading from his early sermons, denouncing his doctrine, questioning his character.

When it was over, the pro-Whitefield minister could stand it no longer. He stood and announced to all that Whitefield would preach a response in half an hour. The crowd was electrified with excitement, "a nice, rough theological thunderstorm being dearly loved in Scotland."[170]

When the time came, Whitefield mounted the pulpit. People were giddy with anticipation. What a treat! The most powerful orator in the land given opportunity to lambaste a critic but thirty minutes after insult and to the same crowd. It would be a verbal bombardment not to be missed!

But it was not to be. Whitefield preached a gospel message not even mentioning Bisset at first. The crowd waited for the thunder to roll, for the rhetorical cannon to fire. Whitefield resisted, simply preaching the word and pleading for weary souls to find their rest. Then, almost as an aside, he remarked, "Had good Mr. Bisset read some of my later writings, wherein I correct several of my former mistakes, he would not have expressed himself in such terms."[171] The sermon resumed while the crowd stood aghast, slowly realizing what the true message of the day had been.

The next morning the city leaders summoned Whitefield and publicly apologized for Bisset's outburst. He was welcome among them, they said, pleased as they were that a man of such character had graced their town and their lives.

This was the trait Whitefield's friends most remembered about him, this big-hearted, compassionate approach to the foibles of men. He confronted human weakness with understanding, rarely punishing or humiliating. The most wounding assault or vilest insult met with gentleness and forgiveness.

This grew first from what he found when he peered into his own soul. He knew his own sinfulness. He knew how often his own unrestrained passions had damaged others, how often he was arrogant or stubborn or low. But he knew from Scripture that the filth of his own heart was merely part of the larger cesspool of all mankind. Men are fallen, marred, far removed from the pure image of God in which they were made. Since folly is common to all men, to rage against the imperfections of a fellow human is both to show ignorance of biblical truth and to spread the muck of human depravity even further.

This worldview made Whitefield an exceptional man. It first made him transparent. Since there was no evil in him but what was common in all men, why should he hide the truth about himself? Perhaps honesty about his own struggles would serve to strengthen others in their times of trial. This openness made Whitefield's *Journals* among the most widely read and revolutionary literature of his time. In fact, they are enduring classics and largely because a respected leader granted a surprisingly open view of his innermost trials and failings. This transparency has inspired generations of leaders—from Finney to Spurgeon to Billy Graham—and largely because Whitefield's openness offered them the very springs of refreshing he had discovered in his times of hardship.

This understanding of man also made him forgiving. He seemed to look with tender reflection upon the assaults against him, as though he knew what it was in a man that made him lash out with venom and hate. Time and again his first response to offense was prayer. His assistants were amazed at how many times they were called together to intercede for one who had just done them harm. They were also amazed at how many times a vicious opponent was transformed into an adoring friend by the soft answer that turns away wrath, by the blessing that Whitefield seemed ever ready to dispense to his enemies.

Finally, this compassionate acceptance of human nature made him generous. He could castigate Harvard for its errant ways, realize his error, and then raise money for the rebuilding of the school's library after a fire. He could suffer lifelong injury from a man and then be found the only one at the same man's deathbed, lovingly tending his former enemy to the last breath. He could be attacked and nearly killed by a crowd of angry villagers and then turn and build a school for the children of that same crowd. Such kindness is possible only for those who know the failings of men and regard that knowledge as a call to compassion and forgiveness.

After so many millennia of human experience, what ought to surprise us about human nature is that we are so surprised about human nature. Men are fallen. They are flawed, often cruel, most always weak.

But they are also made in the image of God. George Whitefield knew that if there was any hope for mankind it was in drawing out that marred image and building on it. It is what stood him apart from lesser men in his age and it is what left for generations to come his legacy of the "Greatheart."

SLAVERY

"I went, as my usual custom is, among the Negroes . . . One man was sick in bed, and two of his children said their prayers after me very well. This more and more convinces me that Negro children, if early brought up in the nurture and admonition of the Lord, would make as great proficiency as any white people's children." [172]

*H*OW WONDERFUL it would be if history fell into nice, neat categories. It would be so much easier if heroes were never flawed or the truth always shone bright against the lie. If good and evil never mixed, the past would be such a better place. But history doesn't come in black and white. It comes in shades of gray . . . just like human nature.

This troubling matter of human nature creates an astonishing mess. It enables men to do one thing while believing another. They can kill their neighbors in the name of peace, steal to preserve property, and oppress in the name of democracy. They can preach a truth but live its opposite. Thus the compromising power of human nature.

Not surprisingly, George Whitefield was human; he, too, possessed a troubling capacity for compromise. Nowhere is this more evident than in his views about slavery.

On the one hand, Whitefield passionately opposed the cruelty of American chattel slavery. When he first encountered it in America, he was appalled. He angrily rebuked slaveholders in a fiery letter that was reprinted throughout the colonies. Writing in 1740, he stormed, "Your dogs are caressed and fondled at your tables; but your slaves, who are frequently styled dogs or beasts, have not an equal privilege. They are scarce permitted to pick up the crumbs which fall from their masters' tables . . . Although I pray God the slaves may never be permitted to get the upper hand, yet should such a thing be permitted by Providence, all good men must acknowledge the judgment would be just."[173]

But Whitefield did more than write letters. He deliberately left white Christians waiting while he preached to their slaves. He met often with blacks in private, addressed them publicly in his meetings, and raged against the lie that blacks had no souls. He raised money for Negro schools and chastised slaveholders for neglecting to teach their slaves about Christ. His time with blacks assured him that "their consciences are awake and consequently prepared in good measure for hearing the gospel."[174] He couldn't understand the callousness of Christians who would deny a fellow man the good news.

Slaves, in turn, cheered Whitefield as their champion. Negro poetess Phyllis Wheately urged, "Take him ye Africans, he longs for you: Impartial Savior is his title due."[175] One oft-told story captures the love of many blacks for the famous evangelist. When Whitefield once lay near death in a Portsmouth home, an old Negro woman begged to see him. Word of her request was carried to Whitefield who nodded that she should be brought to him. The aged woman entered his room and sat on the floor, praying and peering intently into his eyes. Finally, she whispered "Master, you just go to heaven's gate. But Jesus Christ said, Get you down; you must not come here yet but go first, and call some more poor Negroes."[176] Within hours, Whitefield was well.

If the story ended there, Whitefield might be listed among the greatest champions of the anti-slavery cause. Sadly, that troubling matter of human nature wouldn't allow it. In 1747, Whitefield found his Georgia orphanage financially troubled and he thought he knew why: Georgia forbade slavery. "The constitution of that colony is very bad," he complained, "and it is impossible for the inhabitants to subsist without the use of slaves." He decided to permit some friends from another state, one that allowed slavery, to purchase for him "a plantation and slaves, which I propose to devote to the support of Bethesda . . . One Negro has been given me. Some more I purpose to purchase this week." The great preacher became a slaveholder and quickly joined the fight for slavery in Georgia. Clearly, his concern for orphans outweighed his concern for slaves: "Had Negroes been allowed, I should not have had a sufficiency to support a great many orphans without expending above half the sum that has been laid out."[177]

It is a troubling memory. One wonders how history might have changed had Whitefield done all in his power to rid the earth of this horrid practice. What might the most famous man in the world have achieved had he lived consistently? Some might have argued that Whitefield only kept in step with his times, that only one denomination—the Quakers—had declared slavery a sin at the time. Even the Bible seems to encourage the practice, some might argue. But it is not enough. Scripture knows nothing of enslaving a man because of the color of his skin. Old Testament laws permit enslaving a conquered enemy or a man who defaults on his debts but never does Scripture permit the kidnappings, the family destruction, or the enforced suffering of the American slave trade. Whitefield ought to have known—and opposed.

It is one of the marvels of history that we learn from both the greatness and the wickedness of mankind. God chooses to speak through both and the wise, those who allow history to free them from their lesser selves, will listen well. But it is never easy. George Whitefield was a great and Godly man. George Whitefield loved black people. George Whitefield owned slaves. There is no avoiding the tension, the disturbing dichotomy. There is only to learn and to know that human nature makes men heroes as surely as it makes them cowards. We must listen, we must learn, and we must rise above.

KNOWLEDGE

"It is better to be a saint than a scholar; indeed, the only way to be a true scholar is to be striving to be a true saint." [178]

I T WAS killing the church. It left congregations dead, ministers proud, and nations unreached. Knowledge alone. Knowledge apart from faith. Dusty landscapes of learning void of life. It was religion of the mind disconnected from the heart. It was knowledge apart from relationship, information without belief. Ministers regurgitated what they had learned in university and their people nodded assent but remained unchanged. Sadder still, they thought themselves righteous for what they knew when, in fact, what they knew kept them from true righteousness.

This was the bondage of the church in Whitefield's day. Men thought they were Christian because they understood Christianity. Ministers fed this deception by donning their learning as a cloak of righteousness. Already, ordination and graduation were virtually the same. Already scholarship was the path of advancement in the church hierarchy: not piety, not prayer or fasting or obedience or spiritual gift. No, men rose by publishing and polish. No wonder the church was weaker than it had been in generations.

It was an agonizing state for a man with the message of the new birth burning within him. Whitefield wanted learning, but he wanted it inspired. He wanted doctrine, but doctrine aflame. He wanted Spirit-empowered learning proclaimed by Spirit-filled men to reap a Spirit-awakened harvest of souls. He wanted the fruits of prayer and fasting and the well-tended soul to join with the fruits of knowledge to revive the church and transform the nation.

As a man of learning and faith himself, he knew it was possible but it seemed almost heretical to the church of his day. This was, after all, a church that doubted whether men had to be born again to preach the gospel. Surely, knowing the truth was enough. How much a man might believe it couldn't matter, could it? A man's heart was his own affair, but if he could preach the homily and minister the sacraments with skill, then he must be qualified. This was both the reasoning, and the bondage, of the day.

Whitefield knew the enemy when he saw it and insisted that "learning without Piety will only render ministers more capable of promoting the Kingdom of the Devil."[179] Knowing that "a dead ministry will always make a dead people," he roared against the clergy of his day. After speaking to a group of ministers who denied the role of experience in religion, he wrote, "Poor Men! I pitied and told them how they rested in learning falsely so called while they were strangers to the power of godliness in their hearts."[180] His journals are filled with reports of revival success which are often followed with sentences like, "This, I know, is foolishness to the natural and the letter-learned men, but I write this for the comfort of God's children."[181] The "letter-learned" didn't miss the insult.

Refusing to simply curse old wineskins, though, Whitefield dreamed of fashioning new ones. He decided to go to the source of the problem and build new schools that would merge knowledge and faith in a vibrant, effective way. He wanted the curriculum to reflect the glory of Christ. When remembering the beautiful Christopher Wren architecture of the College of William and Mary, Whitefield remarked, "I rejoiced in seeing such a place in America. It may be of excellent use, if learning Christ be made one end of their studies, and arts and sciences only introduced and pursued as subservient to that. For want of this, most of our English schools and Universities have sunk into mere seminaries of paganism."[182] Math and literature, history and languages would all be taught so as to feed faith in Jesus and serve the cause of Christendom.

Yet, the instruction had to go outside the classroom, had to be drawn from an encounter with the real world. Speaking of how Christ sent his disciples abroad to learn by doing, Whitefield wrote, "Would the Heads and

Tutors of our Universities but follow His example, and instead of discouraging their pupils from doing anything of this nature, send them to visit the sick and the prisoners, and to pray with and read practical books of religion to the poor, they would find such exercises of more service to them and the Church of God than all their private and public lectures put together."[183] Whitefield's school would merge study and service, lecture and lifting the burdens of others. This is how he would fashion useful ministers and not the robed academics the schools had long produced.

Though Whitefield contributed to the founding of both Princeton and the University of Pennsylvania, he never built the school of his dreams. That remained for future generations. Yet, he did contend for the vision that made those schools possible. Only heaven will reveal the fruit of this vision, but even on earth names like Graham, Moody, Spurgeon, Wilberforce, and Witherspoon speak of a legacy of learned spirituality that Whitefield won for generations after.

AMERICA

*"America, in my opinion, is an excellent
school to learn Christ in."* [184]

T HE TALES of America stirred his imagination. The stories of Jamestown and Plymouth, of Pilgrims and Puritans and settlements in the wilderness, played in his mind. He remembered the vision: "To be a stepping stone of the light of Christ," to live "for the glory of God and the advancement of the Christian faith." It was inspiring. He recalled the words of Herbert: "Religion stands a tiptoe in our land, Ready to pass to the American strand." [185] Both poem and prophecy, the words planted vision in his heart and he couldn't wait to see the land of this holy dream.

When he arrived in America, he was shocked. The smoldering embers of faith survived but they were far less than the spiritual blaze that arrived with the first settlers. Deism, the religion of God as a distant landlord, had done its work. The country wore religion like a loose garment, for convenience and appearance but certainly nothing held dear. He was grieved. He noted in one place evidence of a "praying ministry" from years gone by, but little had survived. Luxury and comfort ruled. He searched for some sign of the forefathers in the faces of their children. One old gentlemen, "looked like a good old Puritan, and gave me an idea of what stamp those men were, who first settled in New England."[186] But it was all shadow and ghost. Little of those lions of God remained.

So, he mourned the passing dream and he prayed. But it wouldn't die. It kept surfacing in his heart, intruding upon his mind. He listened with quiet interest to the people of New England, to the unwitting heirs of the vision: "It often refreshed my soul to hear of the faith of their good forefathers, who first settled in these parts. Notwithstanding they had their foibles, surely they were a set of righteous men."[187]

He walked the land, read the old words, and listened for the heartbeat of God. Then he heard it. That call, that plea to a new generation. And he knew it was time. He knew that "America is to be my chief scene of action."[188]

He set his heart to renew the land. He preached the Word of the Lord but all along knew he was awakening a spirit from another time. He urged them to recall the former days, to "imitate the piety of their forefathers," and to remember who they truly were.[189] Many heard and understood. One newspaper recognized Whitefield's "intermingling of past and present."[190] A New England evangelist affirmed that what Whitefield preached were "the doctrines of the martyrs and other reformers, which were the same our forefathers brought over hither."[191] For Whitefield this was merely the "good old way" aflame, brought home afresh to a generation squandering its heritage in ignorance.

Souls were saved, churches revived, and the founding vision was recovered. Whitefield had awakened the Puritan spirit. Men reclaimed who they truly were in this new land. They rallied to the resurgent vision, no longer individuals but now a nation in spirit. Whitefield had longed to "set all America in a blaze for God" and now it was happening.[192] He reported that "every day I had convincing proof that a blessed Gospel fire had been kindled in the hearts both of ministers and people."[193] And, in time, he found his own heart kindled with love for this new land: "America, I am afraid, begins to be too dear to me."[194]

When the great war of independence arose between Britain and her colonies, Whitefield had been dead for half a decade. Still, the patriots who pressed their case and fought to free a nation's destiny understood who had set them on their course. It was Whitefield who turned them to their fathers, Whitefield who taught them who they were, and Whitefield who showed them what they might be. So, as the early skirmishes of war began, many knew what Phyllis Wheatley, the African poetess, later wrote:

> *When his Americans were burden'd sore*
> *When streets were crimson'd with their guiltless gore*
> *Unrival'd friendship in his breast now strove*
> *The fruit thereof was charity and love*
> *Towards America.*[195]

HUMOR

Opposing clergyman: "I'm sorry to see you here."
Whitefield: "So is the devil." [196]

I T WAS an age when religion was judged by its sobriety, when humor was suspect, and when a clergyman called "dour" would have taken it as a compliment. The word fun was hardly in existence. A joke in a sermon usually meant that the minister was drunk. Laughing in church could get you thrown out, fined, or put in stocks.

George Whitefield knew it was time for a change. Why should laughter be reserved for taverns? Why should a drunk man alone make merry and laugh aloud without giving offense? If God gives true joy, then Christians ought to be the happiest of all people. What is more, how can a people be reached with the humorless, hard-edged approach of most sermons? Surely, God would be pleased to empower his servants with joy, to reach a weary people through vessels who know the lightness of life as well as its heavy load. So believed Whitefield and so he lived.

But not everyone was convinced. William Tennent went to meet the esteemed Rev. Whitefield at the home of a friend. When he arrived he heard Whitefield laughing uproariously from an inner room and wondered if God could use someone so—happy.[197] John Wesley's closest associates were solemn men who questioned whether Whitefield's effusive joy didn't lead him into "jesting which is not convenient."[198] Whitefield didn't seem to care, nor did the children who flocked to him in towns or on shipboard, reveling in his contagious happiness. How many hard-hearted Christians must have shaken their heads in disapproval at the young clergyman, appropriately attired in black robe and wig, playing with the giggling children in the streets and allowing them to hide under his flowing gown.[199]

For the burdened British masses, Whitefield's loving humor was a refreshing change. He could open a sermon to black-faced miners with a funny story and win their hearts. He could also turn most any potentially distracting incident during a sermon into a tool of his message. Once when Whitefield was preaching, he noticed the crowd giggling at something behind him. He turned to find a child mimicking his every move. Whitefield continued, as did the child. Finally, without missing a step in his sermon, Whitefield gestured to the child and said, "Even he may yet be the subject of free and resistless grace!" The crowd howled, as much for the astonishingly easy-going style of the minister as for the small bit of humor.

Sometimes Whitefield's humor rescued the moment from near disaster. During an open-air meeting at Moorfields, one man was so intent on disrupting the meeting that he climbed a tree near the pulpit, dropped his pants, and exposed his private parts. This failing to break up the meeting, the man began urinating toward the pulpit. Whitefield remained unshaken, though this was an obscenity surprising even for 1742. He turned to the crowd, and speaking as though it was the next point of his sermon, said, "Now, am I wrong when I say . . . that man is half a devil and half a beast?" The crowd exploded with laughter and the day was saved.[200]

Whitefield also used humor to reach his friends in the upper levels of society. On one occasion, Benjamin Franklin shared with Whitefield an epitaph he wrote for himself when he was still young. It read: "The Body of B. Franklin, Printer; Like the cover of an old book, its contents torn out, and stripped of its lettering and gilding, lies here, food for worms. But the work shall not be wholly lost. For it will, as he believed, appear once more, in a new and more perfect Edition, corrected and amended by the Author." Whitefield didn't miss a beat. Combining the evangelist's call with a touch of the dry humor a Franklin would appreciate, he fired back, "I have seen your Epitaph. Believe on Jesus, and get a feeling possession of God in your Heart, and you cannot possibly be disappointed of your expected second edition, finely corrected and infinitely amended."[201]

With small steps such as these, Whitefield transformed the sour image of the minister. He would do whatever he must to reach the human heart, but his humor had more than a practical purpose. It was the natural overflow of a joyous relationship with God, of a man who takes God very seriously but never himself. Friends knew this was true the time a drunken man approached Whitefield and said, "Don't you know me? Why, you converted me ten years ago." Whitefield smiled lovingly and said, "I should not wonder. You look like one of *my* converts. If the Lord had converted you, you would be sober now."[202]

DEATH

"How ought creatures to live who are every moment liable to be hurried away by death to judgment." [203]

CHARLES WESLEY called him "a modest, pensive youth." This is Whitefield the Oxford student. It is not hard to imagine him, trudging from his own college, Pembroke, across the street to the grounds of Christ Church. His clothes are worn, his wig untended, his face sunken from the draw of many fasts. His scurrying feet echo on the ancient stone as he enters the quad and makes for the cathedral.

Entering, he sits and lifts his eyes to drink in the meaning of the great gothic house, every adornment intended to speak eternal truth to fallen man. His eyes pass over the windows, down the intricately masoned buttresses, and to the finely carved columns. He sees there what we might imagine were favorite images. They are skulls, carefully crafted to draw the eye aloft and yet return the onlooker's stare with a piercing blankness. They are designed as sermons in stone, a daunting image for an illiterate age. They silently call men to dispel the pressing and the immediate with a contemplation of mortality.

Though Whitefield is barely twenty, he peers intently into the meaning of these hollow faces. A Scripture comes to mind: "Death is the destiny of all men and the living should take this to heart." They are the words of the Preacher in Ecclesiastes, not intended to encourage morbidity or suicide but to move men to think of their lives from the grave. For Whitefield, the Preacher's words and the staring skulls serve as a tuning fork, the steady tone of death that enables him to align his life with its highest meaning.

The lessons of these silent stone faces remained with Whitefield all his life. The thought of death became a razor that cut away the superfluous and the vain to free him for the higher call. He didn't yearn for death in some depressed, escapist fashion. Instead, he anticipated it with the eagerness of one who will see a lost love when it comes, with the hope of one who seeks to honor death by the way he lives.

When Whitefield was twenty-three, he had an experience that deepened the imprint of the stony skulls. He was on the isle of Gibraltar when he was summoned to pray with a dying soldier. Though the "King of Terrors" approached, the man welcomed it, eager to see his Redeemer and singing psalms to hasten the moment. Surprisingly, the man recovered, but his descent toward death never left Whitefield. He saw that a man might so live as to meet death with joy, both for the destiny fulfilled and for the eternity gained. His mention of this in his journal ends with the prayer, "Lord, let me die the death of the righteous, and let my future state be like his."[204]

It would not have been hard for a man in White-field's time to contemplate his death often. The mortality rates were high. Death was a daily presence. Disease, wars, primitive medicine, and the very public punishment of criminals all pressed death into the mind. White-field once wrote with a sigh, "the more I see of the world, the more I grow sick of it every day."[205] Yet, his thoughts about death were beyond mere resignation. The issue wasn't that he would die, but what his death would mean. He challenged himself to live from the vantage point of the grave and to allow the looming shadow of death to move him to greater deeds for his Lord. Sometimes he thought about it in much detail. One smiles to read him wish aloud, "I hope yet to die in the pulpit, or soon after I come out of it."[206]

Indeed, he sometimes went too far. At a dinner gathering of ministers in New Jersey, Whitefield talked joyfully of dying soon and what glory he would see. All the gathered clergymen chimed in their agreement. Except one: William Tennent. Whitefield asked the older Tennent if he looked with eagerness upon death. But the elder man replied, "I have no wish about it!" Whitefield expressed his surprise, but Tennent fired back, "No sir, it is no pleasure to me at all. And if you knew your duty it would be none to you, Brother Whitefield. I have nothing to do with death. My business is to live as long as I can, and as well as I can."

The younger men were astonished. Whitefield pressed again, only to meet one of the soundest rebukes of his life.

"Sir," said Tennent solemnly, "I have no choice about it. I am God's servant and have engaged to do this business as long as he pleases. Let me ask you a question, Brother Whitefield. What do you think I would say if I sent my man Tom into the field to plough, and at noon I found him lounging under a tree and he complained, 'Master, the sun is hot, and the ploughing hard and I am weary. Master, please let me go home!' Why, I would answer he was a lazy fellow and he should do the work I had given him until I pleased to call him home."[207]

Whitefield listened and received the sharp jab intended to correct his course. He still awaited death with joy, but he also left the manner to God and lived as a man who would assure a passing of honor. More simply, he let the tuning fork of death make possible a more beautiful psalm of life.

PART 3:
THE HEROIC LEGACY OF
GEORGE WHITEFIELD

"When I die, the only epitaph that I desire to be engraved upon my tombstone is 'Here lies George Whitefield; what sort of man he was the great day will discover.'" [1]

"A new set of instruments seem to be rising up, by whom, I trust, those that were first sent forth will not only be succeeded, but eclipsed, as the stars are succeeded and eclipsed by the rising sun." [2]

Forgotten Founding Father

I T WAS a bold plan. It had been rolling around Benjamin Franklin's brain for some time. He was getting older and thinking more about his mortality, his legacy. He wanted to do something that would last. And he knew who he wanted to do it with: George Whitefield.

He hadn't always been so sure about the great evangelist. Whitefield was the source of intense excitement throughout the colonies and Franklin, always suspicious of popular whim, definitely had his doubts at first. But then he went to hear the man . . . and those doubts dissolved. He found that Whitefield was neither the screaming fanatic nor the drone of dry doctrine that most preachers were. This man was the real article, an ambassador of God with gifts to match his message. "There is hardly another minister of the Gospel alive who can so bring to life the truth and relevancy of the Scriptures." Franklin wrote; "Almost he persuadeth me to believe."[3]

Yet, for Franklin, there had to be more. Did the man have a soul, he wondered? Was he capable of engaging one on one or did he only come alive in public? In other words, was he as genuinely warm and human as he appeared to be? In time, Franklin found out: "He is a fine conversationalist and a sympathetic listener. He is an ideal friend."[4] The good Dr. Franklin was hooked.

So he wrote Whitefield to win him to the dreams of his latter days. In the usual Franklin style, he began gently, wooing rather than selling: "Life, like a dramatic piece, should . . . finish handsomely. Being now in the last act, I began to cast about for something fit to end with."

Then, ever the diplomat, he wrote, "I sometimes wish, that you and I were jointly employ'd by the Crown to settle a colony on the Ohio . . . to settle in that fine country a strong body of religious and industrious people."[5] How fascinating: Franklin wanted to start a colony across the mountains in the Tennessee and Ohio regions.

It might work, but why did he need Whitefield? What would America's premier statesman need with a British preacher? Franklin explained: "Might it not greatly facilitate the introduction of pure religion among the heathen, if we could, by such a colony, show them a better sample of Christians than they commonly see in our Indian traders?"[6]

So that was it. Franklin the rationalist, Franklin the ever ardent Deist, might not accept biblical Christianity as true, but he sure knew what it took to settle the wilderness. He knew that success on the frontier took courage, morality, community, devotion to duty—all the virtues that faith provides. He knew, also, that the Indians of the west would only be won with "a better sample of Christians." And what better man to make such Christians and win the west for God than George Whitefield—his friend, his business partner, and the greatest preacher since Jesus Christ.

It was a brilliant plan and, though it never came about, it showed how much Franklin gave homage to the character and message of George Whitefield.

But Franklin was not alone. The truth is that the entire founding generation of Americans felt the same way. Whitefield was, to put it simply, God's man for their times and every man and woman in the colonies seemed to know it.

Certainly their leaders did. Consider what George Washington said of Whitefield: "Upon his lips the Gospel appears even to the coarsest of men as sweet and as true as, in fact, it is."[7]

Then there is the testimony of John Adams: "I know of no philosopher, or theologian, or moralist, ancient or modern, more profound, more infallible than Whitefield."[8]

And, ever the chiding orator, Patrick Henry challenged: "Would that every bearer of God's glad tidings be as fit a vessel of grace as Mr. Whitefield."[9]

The founding fathers' praise for George Whitefield could fill volumes. Indeed, it is not going too far to say that Whitefield was the most beloved man in the colonies.

Yet, Americans today must remember that Americans of old loved Whitefield not just for his transforming ministry and his labors for the poor, but also because he risked all to protect their liberties, as we have seen. Long before most colonial leaders understood and when he might have been arrested for doing so, Whitefield warned the colonies of the schemes of King and Parliament and urged them to stand in the strength of their newly awakened sense of destiny. Consider Whitefield's urgent plea to the leading ministers of Portsmouth. It dates from 1764 and is typical of similar warnings he gave throughout the colonies. Note the compassion, the tender devotion to the cause of America.

> I can't in conscience leave the town without acquainting you with a secret. My heart bleeds for America. O poor New England! There is a deep laid plot against both your civil and religious liberties, and they will be lost. Your golden days are at an end. You have nothing but trouble before you.[10]

With similar pleas, Whitefield sounded the alarm throughout the colonies, much as Paul Revere and Richard Dawes would do on their famous rides some years later. A sleeping people had to be awakened and roused to their defense. So now the forerunner of the revival that made them one became the forerunner of the war that set them free. It is why men marched into battle chanting: "No King but King Jesus! No King but King Jesus." It is why they pledged to God their lives, their fortunes, and their sacred honor. It is also why George Whitefield must be remembered as a founding father of the American cause.

Yet, beyond the shores of America, Whitefield was father to so much more. It cannot be denied, for instance, that Whitefield was father to the Methodist movement and thus to much of the good that movement has accomplished in the world. This is in no way to diminish John Wesley, whose organizational gifts and doctrinal clarity gave to Methodism what it would never have had under Whitefield alone. These gifts, and the fact that Wesley outlived Whitefield by more than twenty years, have assured that Wesley would be the more remembered of the two, and perhaps rightly so.

Still, it was Whitefield who first "experienced" Jesus Christ in a way that the coming revivals offered to millions, and Whitefield who first formed a Methodist "society." It was also Whitefield whom God used to spark revival among the masses, Whitefield who first preached out of doors, and Whitefield who first began reaching across the divisions of the body of Christ. Though no one would be less pleased than Whitefield were a rivalry set up between him and Wesley some two centuries after his death, the fact is that those who have drunk deep of the rich legacy of Methodism owe much to God's use of George Whitefield.

The same is true of those who have eaten the fruits of spiritual revival since Whitefield's time. It is not going too far to say that Whitefield practically invented the modern revival. Consider his many innovations. He organized mass meetings to reach the lost, employed "advance teams" to great effect, and used the full power of the press to proclaim the news of God's work. It had never been done before. But there was more. He organized conferences, published a magazine, connected social projects to the work of revival, and instituted methods of "follow-up" to assure the growth and nurture of converts.

Others followed in his wake. Charles Finney, the great American revivalist of the early 1800's, made Whitefield's methods his own. Though Finney rejected Whitefield's Calvinism, he understood that in the 1740's "the church in New England had enjoyed little else than Arminian preaching, and all were resting in themselves and their own strength."[11] Whitefield was right to inject a dose of God's sovereignty, Finney believed, and hailed him as an "innovator" whose "new measures" were the key to reaching masses for Christ. In following his mentor, Finney's preaching led to an estimated five hundred thousand conversions in the years before the American Civil War.

There were still others. Charles Spurgeon, the eminent Victorian pastor and writer, read Whitefield's *Journals* again and again throughout his life and was profoundly shaped by his methods. Spurgeon, who is often called the "Prince of Preachers," once admitted, "My own model, if I may have such a thing in due subordination to my Lord, is George Whitefield. But with unequal footsteps must I follow in his glorious track."[12]

Dwight Moody also used many of Whitefield's methods to reach the burgeoning cities of post-Civil War America. Linking commerce to the cause of Christ, Moody urged businessmen to see their profits as tools of revival. He passed out donation cards in his meetings, used highly trained advance teams, employed the power of advertising with astonishing success, and built institutions to sustain the work of his ministry. Many of these survive until this day—Moody Press, Moody Bible Institute, and Moody Radio Network are but a few.

There were others, such as Billy Sunday, Oral Roberts, and Billy Graham. Each of these built on the foundation laid by Whitefield while making their own unique contributions along the way. One built a major university. Another spoke to millions by satellite. Yet each in his own way fulfilled the dream of George Whitefield: that every method, every tool, and every resource be used to spread the transforming gospel of Jesus. Truly, the world has never since been the same.

So he was father to a nation, father to a movement, and father to a means of spreading spiritual power. Still, we must remember the individuals, the solitary lives whom he also fathered as he spoke the truth of God.

There was, for example, the ten-year-old boy who once heard him speak. The year was 1769 and Whitefield was preaching the last sermon he would ever preach in England. The boy listened intently, and as he did, he felt something eternal stamped upon his soul. In time, the imprint dimmed as the boy became a man and threw himself into the ways of the world. Later, as he traveled in Italy, he happened to pick up a hotel copy of Philip Doddridge's *The Rise and Progress of Religion.* As he read it his heart melted. All that Whitefield had preached those many years before came roaring back and the young man gave his life to God. His name was William Wilberforce and one day he would almost single-handedly drive slavery out of the British Empire.

There were others of great fame whom Whitefield touched. There was the hymn writer John Newton, who thought Whitefield the greatest preacher who ever lived. John Witherspoon, president of Princeton and signer of the Declaration of Independence, never ceased to acknowledge Whitefield's deep impact on his life. Nor did Jonathan Edwards, dean of American theologians, who never forgot the power of Whitefield in his Northampton pulpit. There is no way to know them all, but the list of the great whom Whitefield influenced would include poets like Phyllis Wheatley, statesmen like James Madison, and firebrands like Patrick Henry.

Yet there are hundreds whose names we will never know, for Whitefield touched their lives through his amazing gift for friendship. He befriended those of every class, race, and station. He drew close to him fellow ministers and butchers, printers and the nobles of the realm. Even John Wesley, whose friendship with Whitefield was often on shaky ground, understood that he "had a heart susceptible of the most generous and the most tender friendship. I have frequently thought that this, of all others, was the distinguishing part of his character. How few have we known of so kind a temper, of such large and flowing affections. Was it not principally by this that the hearts of others were drawn and knit to him? Can anything but love beget love? This shone in his countenance, and continually breathed in his words whether in public or private. Was it not this which quick as lightning, flew from heart to heart, which gave that lift to his sermons, his conversations, his letters?"[13] It may well be said that his capacity for friendship did much to change the world.

It was also changed by the causes he made his own. That he took up the case of the poor in an age grown callous and small has certainly left its mark upon the ages. Some have suggested that the concern for the unfortunate we read in Dickens was first awakened in the British people by the sermons of George Whitefield. It may well be. Few had spoken so boldly of the plight of the poor and few had linked its answer to the heart of true faith as he did. Certainly, the street urchins of London, the orphans of Georgia, and the coal miners of Bristol were never the same after Whitefield and his care for them modeled a muscular brand of Godly compassion that has survived for generations.

It may also be true that Whitefield rescued Calvinism from the narrow, ingrown creature it was becoming in his day. He marveled that the idea of a people chosen by God could produce anything like arrogance or self-importance. For Whitefield, predestination was the greatest reason for humility, obedience, and gratitude. What a wonder that God has chosen to save sinners by His grace! How glorious that preaching is the privilege of harvesting what a man has not planted and cannot grow! This was the glory of Calvinism and Whitefield reveled in it: the freedom from works, the assurance of grace, the boldness of a man held by God. It was Calvinism aflame and Whitefield carried it passionately to the nations.

He may have rescued the cause of revival, as well. He was, after all, a revivalist, a man who loved the moving of God's Spirit and the power of God's Word. Yet he modeled a brand of leadership that protected the pure work of God from every weed that the flesh, the devil, and the world tried to plant. The modern revivalist may be surprised to hear that Whitefield called no one to the altar, did nothing to encourage emotional excitement, and preached that true revival could be measured only by whether people grew increasingly into the likeness of Jesus. As a result, the revivals he led were more powerful, longer lasting, and more deeply transforming than any in history to that time. For Whitefield, revival was the power of God working on the human soul. To insist on more he considered idolatry. To wish for less was backsliding. Thus Whitefield modeled the wise leadership that great works of God demand.

Yet, of all that Whitefield championed, nothing was of greater importance than the fact that he was simply a Christian. To miss this is to miss the essence of White-field. His Christianity was more than cultural, more than a name that comes from joining a movement. It was the passionate pursuit of Jesus Christ. He believed that salvation was the start of a relationship, a personal, transforming experience of Christ within. This made all he did the outgrowth of intimacy and it does much to explain his style and his power. He lost himself in the person of Jesus and it loosened his hold on possessions, reputation, and earthly power. He simply wanted Christ glorified and there is little else that explains why he lived and why he preached as he did.

There is also little else that explains why he held such appeal for those who knew him. People of every class, every color, and every station were drawn to him. It is unexplainable unless it was simply the attraction of men to the mark of the Master upon his life. Benjamin Franklin seemed to be among them, for though he had every reason to distance himself from the preacher, he grew ever more tender as the years went by. Probably, no one was more mystified by it than Franklin himself. Still, as the great evangelist neared death, Franklin sensed it, and wrote to his brother what millions surely echoed in their hearts. "He is a good man," the aging philosopher admitted, "and I love him."

GEORGE WHITEFIELD:
THE LESSONS OF LEADERSHIP

1. Critics are the unpaid guardians of the soul.

2. Humility is the freedom from self that great leadership demands.

3. Suffering purifies the heart, hones the vision, and fashions the soul for battles to come.

4. A truly effective public life is only possible if grown from a truly nourishing private life.

5. Great leaders read in order to lead.

6. Intercessory prayer is the long-range artillery of God. Leadership of eternal consequence is impossible without it.

7. Extremes are deformity of purpose and wise leaders check the one to preserve the other.

8. Applying the past to the present so as to shape the future is the leader's art.

9. To view life from the vantage point of death is to grasp the purpose for living.

10. Leadership is a trust of power on behalf of the poor and the needy.

11. Great leaders welcome hardship as the price of lasting change.

12. The leader who knows he is destined is the leader who can risk in pursuit of a dream.

13. Leaders must conquer the demons of their souls before they can conquer the demons of their age.

14. Great leadership is impossible without great love.

15. Leadership is about values that leaders must live before they proclaim.

16. To offer a people hope is to acquire a position of leadership in their lives.

17. Humor is the celebration of joy that gives life, and thus true leadership, its meaning.

18. To draw out the best that is in a man despite his flaws is to lead him toward the man he is called to be.

19. To make a divided people one in the service of a noble cause is the hallmark of great leadership.

20. Every man has a destiny, but his destiny is fulfilled by investing in the destinies of others.

NOTES

FOREWORD

1. Randy Colver and Cathy Colver, "The Quotable Whitefield," *Christian History*, Issue 38, Vol. XII, No. 2. (Carol Stream, IL: Christianity Today, Inc., 1993), 2.

2. Ibid.

3. John Cullen Morrison, *The Great Evangelists of the Eighteenth Century* (London: Gambel and Price, 1958), 153.

4. James Allen Grant, *George Whitefield in Scotland* (Edinburgh, UK: MacDonald, Kleeve, and Furrows, 1979), 88.

5. Ibid.

6. *Christian History*, XII.

7. Carl Vrestead, *Whitefield* (London: Empire Bible Association, 1936), 44.

8. Ibid.

9. Ibid.

10. Ibid., 90.

11. Ibid.

12. Arnold A. Dallimore, *George Whitefield, The Life and Times of the Great Evangelist of the Eighteenth-Century Revival* Volume II (Westchester, IL: Crossway Books, 1979), 136.

13. Vrestead, 91.

14. Undoubtedly there were a great many innovative evangelists both before and after Whitefield who contributed to modern evangelistic methodology and practice. Whitefield

stands out in innumerable ways. See J. C. Ryle, *Christian Leaders of the Eighteenth Century* (Edinburgh, UK: Banner of Truth Trust, 1978).

15. Again, a great number of notables contributed to the flowering of the Great Awakening. But none more significantly than Whitefield. See John Pollock, *George Whitefield and the Great Awakening* (Tring, UK: Lion, 1972).

16. Though John and Charles Wesley are today known as the founders of Methodism, it was Whitefield who actually enticed them to join his fledgling movement. See Arnold Dallimore, *George Whitefield* (Wheaton, IL: Crossway Books, 1990).

17. The connection between the ideas of Christian liberty exposited by Whitefield and the ideas of political liberty expounded by the Founding Fathers has been ably explored in numerous scholarly works. See Ellis Sandoz, *Political Sermons of the American Founding Era* (Indianapolis, IN: Liberty, 1991).

18. Ibid., 45.

19. Ibid.

20. Ibid.

PART 1: THE HEROIC LIFE OF GEORGE WHITEFIELD

1. Colver and Colver, "The Quotable Whitefield," *Christian History*, 28.

2. George Whitefield, *George Whitefield's Journals* (Edinburgh, Scotland: The Banner of Truth Trust, 1905), 31.

3. Charles Royster, *A Revolutionary People at War: The Continental Army and American Character, 1775–1783* (Chapel Hill: University of North Carolina Press, 1979), 23–24.

4. Charles Dickens, *A Tale of Two Cities* (Minneapolis, MN: Amaranth Press, 1985), 584.

5. Dallimore, 23.

6. Ibid., 28.

7. Ibid.

8. Arnold A. Dallimore, *George Whitefield, The Life and Times of the Great Evangelist of the Eighteenth-Century Revival* Volume I (Westchester, IL: Cornerstone Books, 1970), 25.

9. Albert D. Belden, *George Whitefield—The Awakener* (Nashville, TN: Cokesbury Press, 1930), 55.

10. Ibid.

11. Ibid.

12. John Pollock, *George Whitefield and the Great Awakening* (Herts, England: Lion Publishing, 1972), 25.

13. Ibid., 40.

14. Ibid.

15. Ibid.

16. Ibid.

17. Ibid., 41.

18. Ibid.

19. Ibid.

20. Ibid.

21. Ibid., 42.

22. Ibid., 43.

23. Ibid., 44.

24. Ibid.

25. Pollock, *George Whitefield and the Great Awakening*, 7.

26. Whitefield, *Journals*, 47.

27. Ibid.

28. Ibid.

29. Ibid., 57.

30. Ibid., 58.

31. Ibid., 62.

32. Ibid., 67.

33. Belden, *George Whitefield—The Awakener*, 26.

34. Ibid., 29.

35. Whitefield, *Journals*, 77.

36. Ibid., 79.

37. Ibid.

38. Dallimore, *George Whitefield*, Volume I, 106.

39. Whitefield, *Journals*, 81.

40. Ibid.

41. Ibid.

42. Ibid., 89.

43. Ibid., 83.

44. Ibid., 90.

45. Ibid., 92.

46. Pollock, *George Whitefield and the Great Awakening*, 52.

47. Belden, *George Whitefield—The Awakener*, 43.

48. Whitefield, *Journals*, 119.

49. Pollock, *George Whitefield and the Great Awakening*, 60.

50. Ibid., 60–61.

51. Ibid.

52. Belden, *George Whitefield—The Awakener*, 60.

53. Pollock, *George Whitefield and the Great Awakening*, 79.

54. Ibid., 82.

55. Whitefield, *Journals*, 227.

56. Belden, *George Whitefield—The Awakener*, 68.

57. Ibid., 64.

58. Whitefield, *Journals*, 260.

59. Harry S. Stout, *The Divine Dramatist, George Whitefield and the Rise of Modern Evangelicalism* (Grand Rapids, MI: William B. Eerdmans Publishing Company, 1991), 84.

60. Ibid.

61. Ibid.

62. Ibid.

63. Stout, *The Divine Dramatist*, 90.

64. Ibid.

65. Benjamin Franklin (with Dixon Wecter and Larzer Ziff [editor]), *Benjamin Franklin's Autobiography and Selected Writings* (New York: Holt, Rinehart and Winston, 1967), 107.

66. Ibid., 110.

67. Belden, *George Whitefield—The Awakener*, 81.

68. Ibid., 83.

69. Pollock, *George Whitefield and the Great Awakening*, 125.

70. Dallimore, *George Whitefield*, Volume I, 368.

71. Ibid., 470–76.

72. Stout, *The Divine Dramatist*, 116.

73. Ibid., 126.

74. Stout, *The Divine Dramatist*, 127.

75. Whitefield, *Journals*, 561–62.

76. Stout, *The Divine Dramatist*, 132.

77. John Gillies, *Memoirs of the Life of the Reverend George Whitefield, A.M.* (New Haven: Andrus & Starr, 1812), 48.

78. Pollock, *George Whitefield and the Great Awakening*, 173.

79. J. D. Walsh, "Wesley vs. Whitefield," *Christian History*, Issue 38, Vol. XII, No. 2 (Carol Stream, IL: Christianity Today, Inc., 1993), 34.

80. Pollock, *George Whitefield and the Great Awakening*, 236.

81. Gillies, *Memoirs*, 144.

82. Mark Galli, "Whitefield's Curious Love Life," *Christian History*, Issue 38, Vol. XII, No. 2 (Carol Stream, IL: Christianity Today, Inc., 1993), 33.

83. Ibid.

84. Dallimore, *George Whitefield*, Volume II, 472.

85. Pollock, *George Whitefield and the Great Awakening*, 204.

86. Ibid., 204.

87. Ibid., 205.

88. Ibid., 206.

89. Ibid., 207.

90. Pollock, *George Whitefield and the Great Awakening*, 224.

91. Mark Galli, "Slaveholding Evangelist," *Christian History*, Issue 38, Vol. XII, No. 2 (Carol Stream, IL: Christianity Today, Inc., 1993), 41.

92. Belden, *George Whitefield—The Awakener*, 61.

93. Pollock, *George Whitefield and the Great Awakening*, 231.

94. Ibid., 228.

95. Pollock, *George Whitefield and the Great Awakening*, 239.

96. Frank Lambert, *Pedlar in Divinity, George Whitefield and the Transatlantic Revivals* (Princeton, NJ: Princeton University Press, 1994), 218.
97. Ibid., 219–23.
98. Whitefield, *Journals*, 142.
99. J. C. Ryle, *Christian Leaders of the Eighteenth Century* (Edinburgh, Scotland: The Banner of Truth Trust, 1978), 42.
100. Ibid.
101. Ibid., 42–43.
102. Pollock, *George Whitefield and the Great Awakening*, 271–72.
103. Belden, *George Whitefield—The Awakener*, 224.

PART 2: THE HEROIC CHARACTER OF GEORGE WHITEFIELD

1. Arnold Dallimore, "Pushing to the Point of Exhaustion," *Christian History*, Issue 38, Vol. XII, No 2 (Carol Stream, IL: Christianity Today, Inc., 1993), 28.
2. Colver and Colver, "The Quotable Whitefield," *Christian History*, 28.
3. Whitefield, *Journals*, 241.
4. Ibid., 159–61.
5. Stout, *The Divine Dramatist*, 237.
6. Pollock, *George Whitefield and the Great Awakening*, 147.
7. Kevin A. Miller, "The Original Christian History," *Christian History*, Issue 38, Vol. XII, No. 2 (Carol Stream, IL: Christianity Today, Inc., 1993), 6.
8. Whitefield, *Journals*, 483.
9. Pollock, *George Whitefield and the Great Awakening*, 147.
10. Stout, *The Divine Dramatist*, 130.
11. Whitefield, *Journals*, 429.
12. Ibid., 206.
13. Ibid., 195.

14. Ibid., 462.
15. Ibid., 245.
16. Ibid., 205.
17. Dallimore, *Christian History*, 28.
18. Whitefield, *Journals*, 5.
19. Ibid., 247.
20. Ibid., 396.
21. Ibid., 200.
22. Pollock, *George Whitefield and the Great Awakening*, 246.
23. Whitefield, *Journals*, 179.
24. Ibid., 169.
25. Ibid., 110.
26. Ibid., 79.
27. Ibid., 166.
28. Ibid., 90.
29. Whitefield, *Journals*, 230.
30. Ibid., 234.
31. Stout, *The Divine Dramatist*, 61.
32. Whitefield, *Journals*, 450.
33. Pollock, *George Whitefield and the Great Awakening*, 120.
34. Whitefield, *Journals*, 265.
35. Ibid., 370.
36. Ibid., 233.
37. Whitefield, *Journals*, 133.
38. Pollock, *George Whitefield and the Great Awakening*, 181.
39. Whitefield, *Journals*, 410.
40. Lambert, *Pedlar in Divinity*, 6.
41. Ibid., 46.
42. Ibid., 65.
43. Pollock, *George Whitefield and the Great Awakening*, 80.
44. Whitefield, *Journals*, 209.
45. Belden, *George Whitefield–The Awakener*, 235.
46. Whitefield, *Journals*, 139.
47. Ibid., 124.
48. Ibid., 139.

49. Ibid., 51.
50. Ibid., 262.
51. Ibid., 78.
52. Ibid., 363.
53. Colver and Colver, *Christian History*, 28.
54. Whitefield, *Journals*, 134.
55. Colver and Colver, *Christian History*, 28.
56. Whitefield, *Journals*, 167.
57. Whitefield, *Journals*, 108.
58. Ibid., 107.
59. Ibid., 104.
60. Ibid., 98.
61. Ibid., 483.
62. Ibid.
63. Ibid., 431.
64. Pollock, *George Whitefield and the Great Awakening*, 71.
65. Whitefield, *Journals*, 475.
66. Pollock., *George Whitefield and the Great Awakening*, 66.
67. Whitefield, *Journals*, 253.
68. Ibid., 578.
69. Ibid., 491.
70. Ibid., 62.
71. Ibid., 491.
72. Whitefield, *Journals*, 380–81.
73. Ibid., 310.
74. Ibid., 311.
75. George Grant and Karen Grant, *Best Friends* (Nashville, TN: Cumberland House Publishing, Inc., 1998), *Best Friends*, 54.
76. Ibid., 53.
77. Arnold A. Dallimore, *George Whitefield, The Life and Times of the Great Evangelist of the Eighteenth-Century Revival*, Volume 2 (Westchester, IL: Crossway Books, 1979), 285.
78. Pollock, *George Whitefield and the Great Awakening*, 12.
79. Whitefield, *Journals*, 311.
80. Ibid., 232.

81. Ibid., 43.
82. Ibid., 53–54.
83. 2 Corinthians 2:11, The Holy Bible, New International Version.
84. Whitefield, *Journals*, 370.
85. Ibid., 484.
86. Ibid., 275.
87. Ibid., 233.
88. Ibid., 239.
89. Colver and Colver, *Christian History*, 28.
90. Lambert, *Pedlar in Divinity*, 17.
91. Whitefield, *Journals*, 114.
92. Ibid., 168, 170.
93. Ibid., 171.
94. Ibid., 463.
95. Ibid., 336.
96. Belden, *George Whitefield—The Awakener*, 41–42.
97. Whitefield, *Journals*, 102.
98. Ibid., 123.
99. Ibid., 148.
100. Ibid., 109.
101. Ibid., 167.
102. Ibid.
103. Ibid., 142.
104. Belden, *George Whitefield—The Awakener*, 164.
105. Pollock, *George Whitefield and the Great Awakening*, 131.
106. Ibid., 159.
107. Ibid., 206.
108. Lambert, *Pedlar in Divinity*, 193.
109. Ibid., 80.
110. Pollock, *George Whitefield and the Great Awakening*, 239.
111. Ibid., 208.
112. Colver and Colver, *Christian History*, 28.
113. Stout, *The Divine Dramatist*, 193.
114. Whitefield, *Journals*, 92.
115. Ibid., 60–61.

116. Franklin, 109.
117. Ibid.
118. Whitefield, *Journals*, 144.
119. Lambert, *Pedlar in Divinity*, 37.
120. Whitefield, *Journals*, 305.
121. Ibid., 175.
122. Ibid., 331.
123. Ibid., 116.
124. Ibid., 150.
125. Lambert, *Pedlar in Divinity*, 84.
126. Whitefield, *Journals*, 140.
127. Ibid., 223.
128. Ibid., 175.
129. Ibid., 197.
130. Ibid., 17.
131. Pollock, *George Whitefield and the Great Awakening*, 147.
132. Lambert, *Pedlar in Divinity*, 154.
133. Pollock, *George Whitefield and the Great Awakening*, 249.
134. Ibid., 86.
135. Ibid., 11.
136. Stout, *The Divine Dramatist*, 131.
137. Whitefield, *Journals*, 347–48.
138. Stout, *The Divine Dramatist*, 39.
139. Colver and Colver, *Christian History*, 28.
140. Dallimore, *George Whitefield*, 26.
141. Whitefield, *Journals*, 246.
142. Ibid., 135.
143. Ibid., 86.
144. Belden, *George Whitefield—The Awakener*, 235.
145. Galli, "Whitefield's Curious Love Life," *Christian History*, 33.
146. Jim Bishop, *The Day Lincoln Was Shot* (New York: Gramercy Books, 1983), 24.
147. Ibid., 25.
148. Galli, *Christian History*, 33.
149. Dallimore, *George Whitefield*, Volume I, 368.

150. Galli, *Christian History*, 33.
151. Ibid.
152. Pollock, *George Whitefield and the Great Awakening*, 199.
153. Galli, *Christian History*, 33.
154. Ibid.
155. Whitefield, *Journals*, 15.
156. Jonah 2:8 (NIV).
157. Whitefield, *Journals*, 17.
158. Ibid., 109.
159. Dallimore, *George Whitefield*, Volume II, 188.
160. Dallimore, *George Whitefield*, Volume I, 97.
161. Pollock, *George Whitefield and the Great Awakening*, 28.
162. Whitefield, *Journals*, 136.
163. Belden, *George Whitefield—The Awakener*, 162.
164. "Did You Know?" *Christian History*, Issue 38, Vol. XII, No. 2 (Carol Stream, IL: Christianity Today, Inc., 1993), 3.
165. Gary Sanseri, "House of Mercy, Prison of Debt," *Christian History*, Issue 38, Vol. XII, No. 2 (Carol Stream, IL: Christianity Today, Inc., 1993), 32.
166. Pollock, *George Whitefield and the Great Awakening*, 250.
167. Ibid.
168. Whitefield, *Journals*, 373.
169. Whitefield, *Journals*, 478.
170. Pollock, *George Whitefield and the Great Awakening*, 183.
171. Ibid., 183–84.
172. Whitefield, *Journals*, 379.
173. Galli, "Slaveholding Evangelist," *Christian History*, 41.
174. Ibid.
175. Lambert, *Pedlar in Divinity*, 220.
176. Pollock, *George Whitefield and the Great Awakening*, 215.
177. Galli, "Slaveholding Evangelist," *Christian History*, 41.
178. Colver and Colver, *Christian History*, 28.
179. Lambert, *Pedlar in Divinity*, 19.
180. Whitefield, *Journals*, 210.
181. Ibid., 253.

182. Ibid., 371.

183. Ibid., 70.

184. Whitefield, *Journals*, 165.

185. Ibid., 363.

186. Ibid., 452.

187. Ibid., 482.

188. Pollock, *George Whitefield and the Great Awakening*, 167.

189. Whitefield, *Journals*, 472.

190. Lambert, *Pedlar in Divinity*, 105.

191. Ibid., 24.

192. Pollock, *George Whitefield and the Great Awakening*, 226.

193. Ibid.

194. Ibid.

195. Lambert, *Pedlar in Divinity*, 224.

196. Pollock, *George Whitefield and the Great Awakening*, 158.

197. Ibid., 117.

198. Ibid., 243.

199. Ibid., 130.

200. Ibid., 200.

201. Lambert, *Pedlar in Divinity*, 129.

202. Pollock, *George Whitefield and the Great Awakening*, 250.

203. Whitefield, *Journals*, 138.

204. Ibid., 149.

205. Ibid., 184.

206. Ibid., 199.

207. Pollock, *George Whitefield and the Great Awakening*, 264–65.

PART 3: THE HEROIC LEGACY OF GEORGE WHITEFIELD

1. Colver and Colver, *Christian History*, 28.

2. Whitefield, *Journals*, 31–32.

3. Grant and Grant, *Best Friends*, 56.

4. Ibid.

5. Frank Lambert, "The Religious Odd Couple," *Christian History*, Issue 38, Vol. XII, No. 2 (Carol Stream, IL: Christianity Today, Inc., 1993), 31.

6. Ibid.

7. Grant and Grant, *Best Friends*, 52.

8. Lambert, *Pedlar in Divinity*, 225.

9. Grant and Grant, *Best Friends*, 52.

10. Carl Bridenbaugh, *Mitre and Sceptre, Transatlantic Faiths, Ideas, Personalities, and Politics* (London, England: Oxford University Press, 1962), 244.

11. Lambert, *Pedlar in Divinity*, 228.

12. Whitefield, *Journals*, 5.

13. Pollock, *George Whitefield and the Great Awakening*, 176.

Selected Bibliography

"Did You Know?" *Christian History*, Issue 38, Vol. XII, No. 2 (Carol Stream, IL: Christianity Today, Inc., 1993) 3.

Belden, Albert D. *George Whitefield—The Awakener.* Nashville, TN: Cokesbury Press, 1930.

Bishop, Jim. *The Day Lincoln Was Shot.* New York: Gramercy Books, 1983.

Bridenbaugh, Carl. *Mitre and Sceptre, Transatlantic Faiths, Ideas, Personalities, and Politics.* London, England: Oxford University Press, 1962.

Colver, Randy and Colver, Cathy. "The Quotable Whitefield," *Christian History*, Issue 38, Vol. XII, No. 2. Carol Stream, IL: Christianity Today, Inc., 1993.

Dallimore, Arnold A. *George Whitefield, The Life and Times of the Great Evangelist of the Eighteenth-Century Revival*, Volume I. Westchester, IL: Cornerstone Books, 1970.

Dallimore, Arnold A. *George Whitefield, The Life and Times of the Great Evangelist of the Eighteenth-Century Revival*, Volume II. Westchester, IL: Crossway Books, 1979.

Dallimore, Arnold. "Pushing to the Point of Exhaustion," *Christian History*, Issue 38, Vol. XII, No 2. Carol Stream, IL: Christianity Today, Inc., 1993.

Dickens, Charles. *A Tale of Two Cities*. Minneapolis, MN: Amaranth Press, 1985.

Franklin, Benjamin (with Wecter, Dixon and Ziff, Larzer [editor]). *Benjamin Franklin's Autobiography and Selected Writings*. New York: Holt, Rinehart, and Winston, 1967.

Galli, Mark. "Whitefield's Curious Love Life," *Christian History*, Issue 38, Vol. XII, No. 2. Carol Stream, IL: Christianity Today, Inc., 1993.

Galli, Mark. "Slaveholding Evangelist," *Christian History*, Issue 38, Vol. XII, No. 2. Carol Stream, IL: Christianity Today, Inc., 1993.

Gillies, John. *Memoirs of the Life of the Reverend George Whitefield, A.M.* New Haven: Andrus & Starr, 1812.

Grant, George and Karen Grant. *Best Friends*. Nashville, TN: Cumberland House Publishing, Inc., 1998.

Lambert, Frank. "The Religious Odd Couple," *Christian History*, Issue 38, Vol. XII, No. 2. Carol Stream, IL: Christianity Today, Inc., 1993.

Lambert, Frank. *Pedlar in Divinity, George Whitefield and the Transatlantic Revivals*. Princeton, NJ: Princeton University Press, 1994.

Miller, Kevin A. "The Original Christian History," *Christian History*, Issue 38, Vol. XII, No. 2. Carol Stream, IL: Christianity Today, Inc., 1993.

Pollock, John. *George Whitefield and the Great Awakening*. Herts, England: Lion Publishing, 1972.

Royster, Charles. *A Revolutionary People at War: The Continental Army and American Character, 1775–1783*. Chapel Hill: University of North Carolina Press, 1979.

Ryle, J. C. *Christian Leaders of the Eighteenth Century*. Edinburgh, Scotland: The Banner of Truth Trust, 1978.

Sanseri, Gary. "House of Mercy, Prison of Debt," *Christian History*, Issue 38, Vol. XII, No. 2. Carol Stream, IL: Christianity Today, Inc., 1993.

Stout, Harry S. *The Divine Dramatist, George Whitefield and the Rise of Modern Evangelicalism*. Grand Rapids, MI: William B. Eerdmans Publishing Company, 1991.

Walsh, J. D. "Wesley vs. Whitefield," *Christian History*, Issue 38, Vol. XII, No 2. Carol Stream, IL: Christianity Today, Inc., 1993.

Whitefield, George. *George Whitefield's Journals*. Edinburgh, Scotland: The Banner of Truth Trust, 1905.